Following God

Renewing the Heart... for Women

LIFE PRINCIPLES FROM THE BEATITUDE

Following God

Renewing the Heart... for Women

LIFE PRINCIPLES FROM THE BEATITUDES

A Bible Study by

BARBARA HENRY

Advancing the Ministries of the Gospel

AMG Publishers

God's Word to you is our highest calling.

Following God

RENEWING THE HEART FOR WOMEN: LIFE PRINCIPLES FROM THE BEATITUDES

Published by AMG Publishers. All Rights Reserved.

Second Printing, 2006

ISBN: 0-89957-337-1

Cover design by Jennifer Ross
Layout by Rick Steele
Editing by Jody El-Assadi and Rick Steele

Printed in the United States of America
10 09 08 07 06 –EB– 6 5 4 3 2

This book is dedicated to

David and Rebecca

for their unrelenting
determination to seek renewal

Acknowledgments

Many thanks go to all the women at Green Lake Presbyterian Church who have supported and encouraged me in the writing of this book. Special thanks to the original support group who helped me develop the ideas and direction the study would take: to Anna Van Wechel, Rebecca Morton, Jeanne Gray, Bethany Meeks, Dagney Leonard, Amanda Cumbow, Lindy Reinmuth, and Mary Laiti. I also appreciate the input from others who helped to critique and develop early manuscripts, Eddie Nudelman, Mary Uppinghouse, Bobbie Parks, Nancy Miller, Margie Balcos, Linda Collins, Cheri Dorman, Pam Olson-Murray, Tatiana Sikora, and Sharon Chin. I also acknowledge the help and encouragement I received from my friends at the Northwest Christian Writer's Association, from Judy Bodmer, Lydia Harris, Rosemarie Kowalski, and Barbara Bryden. And finally, I want to thank all my faithful prayer supporters who have held me up before the throne of grace at Women in Prayer, Parish Group, and those who receive and pray for all my email requests.

I owe sincere thanks to each of the women who allowed me to share their stories. Many of them did an excellent job in writing parts of the story themselves. Some asked to have their names changed to protect their privacy. I appreciate all the time they gave, and their patience in the many changes and rewrites we sent back and forth.

Special thanks to my family for giving me the support I have needed as a writer: to my parents, Al and Betty, for sharing their home with me; to Allan for his faithful support; to my children BJ & Dan, Sara & David, Nathan & Rami, and Daniel for their love and encouragement; and to my grandchildren for all the joy they bring to my life.

I am grateful for all the folks at AMG, and want to especially thank Rick Steele for his patience with me and his careful editing. Congratulations again, to Dan Penwell, for receiving the well deserved title of "Editor of the Year."

Most of all I want to acknowledge the Holy Spirit and His work first in changing my own heart over the past fifteen years, and then giving me a deep desire to encourage others to seek change and renewal.

Barbara Henry

About the Author

Barbara Henry received her B.A. in Education from Covenant College and her M.A. in biblical counseling from Colorado Christian University. She has been involved in women's ministries for over thirty years—leading and writing Bible studies for the local church and discipling women. Her passion for equipping others for ministry makes her a popular speaker in churches across America. This is Barbara's second release in AMG Publisher's acclaimed Following God™ Bible study series, following the success of her study *Woman to Woman: Life Principles from Titus 2.*

Barbara has four grown children who all love and serve the Lord. Her daughters, BJ and Sara, both have three children who love their Nana, and bring her great delight. Her sons, Nathan and Daniel, are both pursuing careers in ministry. Additional information and a leader's guide for this title are available on her website:

www.barbarahenry.org

About the Following God Series

Three authors and fellow ministers, Wayne Barber, Eddie Rasnake, and Rick Shepherd, teamed up in 1998 to write a character-based Bible study for AMG Publishers. Their collaboration developed into the title, *Life Principles from the Old Testament*. Since 1998 these same authors and AMG Publishers have produced six more **character-based** studies—each consisting of twelve lessons geared around a five-day study of a particular Bible personality. In 2001, AMG Publishers launched a series of topical studies called the **Following God™ Discipleship Series,** and this release of *Renewing the Heart for Women* by Barbara Henry becomes the eighth title released in this format. Though new studies and authors are being introduced, the interactive study format that readers have come to love remains constant with each new Following God™ release. As new titles and categories are being planned, our focus remains the same: to provide excellent Bible study materials that point people to God's Word in ways that allow them to apply truths to their own lives. More information on this groundbreaking series can be found on the following web page:

www.amgpublishers.com

Preface

Every woman loves a good story. Whether you are a new Christian who has never studied the Bible before or a veteran student of the Word, you will enjoy these up-close-and-personal vignettes of both characters in the Bible and women of today. Their stories will lead to a new understanding of the Beatitudes, and you will see through their examples how God changes our lives and our hearts.

Many women are struggling with depression, anxiety, addictions, and besetting sins and don't understand why life is so difficult. Deep within us all there is a longing to love God more and to care more for others, however, something holds us back. Just when we have conquered one sin that has kept us from love, we discover another one, even more difficult to overcome. Or the old one comes back to haunt us. Rather than continuing the struggle alone, we need to seek God's provision. He wants to do a supernatural work in us, but is waiting for us to cultivate a desire for change.

Recovering alcoholics are a good example of people who want to change. Years ago two men discovered that the principles found in the Beatitudes could lead men and women out of addiction to alcohol. Because they wanted to appeal to everyone, they removed references to Christ or the Holy Spirit and replaced them with "God as you understand Him." The twelve steps of Alcoholics Anonymous have worked to a degree, and millions have found a measure of happiness in their sobriety. Yet as Christians, we know greater joy and freedom is available. This study of the Beatitudes and related Scriptures will take us further with Christ in the power of the Holy Spirit.

In Mark 4:26–29 Jesus shares the "Parable of the Seed," teaching the mystery of spiritual growth. He identifies the seed as the Word of God. We plant the seed by reading, studying, and discussing the Word with openness and readiness to obey. Then we wait for God's Word to grow and change us. *"The kingdom of God is like a man who casts seed upon the soil . . . the seed sprouts up and grows-how he himself does not know."* Mark 4:26–27. The time we spend interacting with the Word of God and in earnest prayer and supplication will have an immeasurable impact on our souls. God will do the supernatural work to bring about the mysterious changes within us.

Through a study of the principles of these eight promises of blessing, God will draw you into a deep relationship with the Trinity where your love for Him outgrows every other love. He will create in you a deep hunger for righteousness that will trump every other hunger. He will show you how to interpret the bad things that happen to you and how to hope for the present and future. You will read stories of how God turned devastating circumstances into peace and joy beyond understanding. Every woman who allowed me to share her story told me she would not trade the sorrow she went through if it meant she would not experience the deeper love of Christ that was revealed in the midst of it. It is like the pain of childbirth soon forgotten as a mother's heart is filled with love for her newborn. It is a taste of heaven.

You will notice in the table of contents that every chapter is about our hearts. I did not intend to write a study about the heart. Actually, I used to have an aversion to this topic because I didn't know what people were talking about. As an analytical thinker, not in touch with my emotions, and frankly, a bit fearful and suspicious when anyone used the term, I tried to avoid it. This, of course, was difficult for me as a Bible teacher since the Bible has so much to say about the heart. I knew I would have to tackle it eventually in this study, because the sixth Beatitude says *"Blessed are the pure in heart"* but early on in my research I discovered every one of them related to our hearts.

One of the classic definitions of the word "heart" is the seat of affections. Used in this context our hearts are that mysterious part of us with which we love. Just as our physical hearts pump life-blood to the rest of the body, our spiritual hearts pump love—the life-giving essence that makes life worth living. Because love involves our will, emotions, affections, desires, imagination, conscience, and mind, all of these are components of our hearts. Heart issues like discontent, denial, rebellion, coveting, selfishness, impurity, conflict, and self-protection are the things that keep our lives from true love and deep lasting blessing.

It is my prayer that this study of the Beatitudes will be used in your life to make you more like Christ. Begin to pray with me today and every day of this study, "Change my heart, O God."

Following Christ,

Barbara Henry

Table of Contents

How to Use This Study

1. **You can do it alone for personal renewal.** But you will find it much richer if you discuss it with other women. The Spirit will reveal different aspects of truth to each woman and the gain you realize will multiply within community. Also, remember James 5:16, *"Confess your sins to one another, and pray for one another, so that you may be healed."* This clearly teaches us our healing somehow comes through community.

2. **Let it be a starting point.** Focus more on the Scripture than my comments or the quotes. God will use this study to the degree we allow His Word to penetrate our lives. Look for other passages that address the topic—read and discuss them, too.

3. **Try to have access to a New American Standard Bible,** since most of the questions are based on the words used in that version. It will be helpful to use other versions as well, but the questions might be a little confusing when the wording is different.

4. **The application question sections at the end of each day's reading** (highlighted by the red "stop" signs) are meant to help you assimilate what you have studied and leave you with things to meditate on throughout your day. These questions are for personal use, to highlight what the Lord may be teaching you or convicting you about. Perhaps what you write in the short space provided may only reflect key ideas you develop more thoroughly in a journal.

5. **Mentors or discussion group leaders will find the Leader's Guide indispensable.** This leader's guide can be downloaded for free from my website: **www.barbarahenry.org**

   Leader's notes include:

   - ✓ instructions for leaders so that they know what to do to fully prepare for each session
   - ✓ information on what leaders should expect in each session
   - ✓ the main point of each lesson
   - ✓ the main objective in each section
   - ✓ additional discussion questions for each passage (A good leader will not simply provide the answers, but ask questions that will guide the women to discover the answers for themselves.)

6. **Decide if you want to use the study as an eight-week, forty-day quest for renewal, or a year-long in-depth study.** There is enough material included, especially if you utilize the Leader's Guide, to stay in this study for 40 weeks. By thorough study and discussion of all the Scripture passages, a group can cover a section a week. If you choose to do it in 8 weeks, the group meetings would probably be a time of sharing highlights from personal study and prayer for one another, rather than a group Bible study that would take the time to discuss each passage together.

Poor Hearts

*"Blessed are the poor in spirit, for theirs
is the kingdom of heaven" (Matthew 5:6)*

No one has what it takes. Twenty years ago I thought I did. My life was nearly perfect. Happily married to a successful doctor, we had four wonderful, obedient children. I was involved in ministry in a church I loved with many good friends. I thought God blessed us because we had done everything right. But then things started "going wrong" as God began to dismantle my world. First, my husband lost his job. Then a church split prompted us to leave our church, causing us to lose many close friends. Soon after, my husband began showing signs of a midlife crisis—the sports car he purchased was just the first of many signs. I kept thinking all these crises were just a test, a trial of my faith that would soon run its course. I considered myself strong enough to withstand the storm.

I tried to maintain as much control as possible, but things were slipping out of my hands. I wondered where God's blessing had gone, and hoped if I had enough faith it would return. Yet, after five years of struggle and defeat, my life as I had known it for twenty years had ended. My circumstances left me hopeless. My husband had left me for another woman and told me it was time for me to get a job to help support the children. I found a minimum wage job but feared it wouldn't be long before I would lose my home, and possibly even my children. I was physically, emotionally, and spiritually bankrupt. Yet real life—real blessing and real faith was just beginning.

Barbara . . .

*. . . blessings through
spiritual poverty*

Word Study
BEATITUDE

Although this word is not found in Scripture itself, it is usually given as the title of the eight statements of blessing Jesus promised the multitude in Matthew 5:3–10. *Webster* defines it as "a state of utmost bliss." If one has been beatified they have been supremely joyful. The goal of this study is that each of us would be beatified by having our hearts renewed by His Spirit.

Poor Hearts

DAY ONE

"Blessed are the poor in spirit, for theirs is the kingdom of heaven. Blessed are those who mourn, for they shall be comforted. Blessed are the gentle, for they shall inherit the earth. Blessed are those who hunger and thirst for righteousness, for they shall be satisfied. Blessed are the merciful, for they shall receive mercy. Blessed are the pure in heart, for they shall see God. Blessed are the peacemakers, for they shall be called sons of God. Blessed are those who have been persecuted for the sake of righteousness, for theirs is the kingdom of heaven."

Matthew 5:3–10

I had to let go of my pride and learn how completely dependent I was on God. The possibility of experiencing "a state of utmost bliss" (see "Beatitude" Word Study in the side margin) now existed because my circumstances and abilities were no longer my ultimate reason for security or joy. God was starting to teach me the meaning of the Beatitudes. The first thing I had to learn was the blessing of being poor in spirit.

God had to show me my spiritual poverty so I would be drawn to Him to meet my ultimate need—a transformed heart. As long as I was feeling self-satisfied and believed my life was blessed because of my own goodness, I was headed for failure. It was not until I came to the end of myself, realizing my hopelessness and helplessness, and turned to Him, with nothing in my hands, that He could begin a work in me to change my heart and life forever.

ABRAHAM—THE NEED OF A COVENANT PARTNER

In the Old Testament, God's first revelation to the father of the nation of Israel was a promise of blessing. Not surprisingly, in the New Testament, Christ's first sermon to His disciples began with eight promises of blessing. This shows God's continuing desire to bless His people. His covenant love is revealed throughout Scripture, and His blessing comes out of that love. Today we are going to take a careful look at the way God dealt with the father of faith and how He formed in him a heart of trust in His promise of blessing.

📖 Read Genesis 12:1–4. How old was Abraham when God made this first covenant promise? What kinds of blessings were included? What do you know about covenants?

_____

_____

_____

_____

_____

In ancient Eastern cultures individuals and communities used covenants to bind themselves to one another. These covenants provided assurance that the participants could always count on their covenant partner to help in time of need. In the same way today, people who recognize their poverty of spirit can choose to be in similar relationships. Helpless and needy people are wise to find security by entering binding agreements and then relying on the help offered. They are far more blessed than those who stubbornly insist on "going it alone." When we don't have what it takes, we need to hook up with someone who can help us.

In today's culture, marriage is the most common illustration of a covenant. Two individuals pledge to be there for each other for life. Another illustration, this one from the not too distant past, is the Native American custom of blood-brotherhood—a solemn friendship established by a ceremony of commingling their blood. Yet the archetype for covenant relationship existed long before mankind ever thought of the concept and is modeled in the Holy Trinity. The love, commitment, and the perfect, harmonious interaction between the three persons of the Godhead reveal the ultimate pattern for covenant life on earth.

📖 Read Genesis 12:10–20. What does this story tell us about Abram's level of trust? Why do you think it was difficult for him to believe God's promise of blessing?

_____

_____

_____

_____

The story of Abraham reveals the amazing fact that God is willing to be a covenant partner with man. It also illustrates how our desire to believe God's promises sometimes wavers. Abram believed he had to protect himself and could not simply rely on God's promised blessing. (Another similar incident is recorded in Genesis 20.) Perhaps he believed the old adage that "God helps those who help themselves." Contrary to popular opinion, this is not a biblical statement. And in the Beatitudes, Jesus teaches us that God helps (and blesses) those who know they are bankrupt and in dire need of a covenant relationship with Christ.

📖 Read Genesis 15. Why do you think God told Abram to shed the blood of the animals? What does it mean that God credited Abram's faith as righteousness? What do you think is the significance of the fact that Abram slept through the covenant ceremony?

_____

_____

_____

_____

This passage is filled with covenant concepts and language. Those who have studied the customs of Abram's day have discovered many parallels God incorporated into this answer to Abram's question in verse 8. When Abram asks, "How may I know that I shall possess it," God gives to Abram the assurance that he could believe in His promises by cutting flesh and shedding blood. God was establishing a covenant according to the custom of the day. Abram would have recognized this ritual as a commitment by God signed in blood that He would be there for Abram and would be faithful to His promises. Years ago I heard Malcolm Smith teach that in the custom of Abram's day, both parties of the covenant would have walked through the divided animals together, thereby sealing their promise of commitment to each other. The idea being, if one breaks a covenant in any way, that person should be cut in half like these animals.[3] The only thing Abram brought to the covenant was his faith. He believed God's promises. It is the same for us. We are saved by faith. We receive the promises of God by faith. We are in covenant with God by faith in the sufficiency of Christ's blood shed for us.

Word Study
POOR IN SPIRIT

The Greek word translated "poor" in Matthew 5:3 is *ptochos,* and it means destitute, beggarly, bankrupt. The Greek word translated spirit in this verse is *pneuma,* which refers to "the sentient element in us, that by which we perceive, reflect, feel, and desire."[1] So to be poor in spirit is to realize our great need for renewal in our perception, our reflections, our feelings, and our desires.

Word Study
COVENANT

- Between nations: a treaty or alliance of friendship
- Between individuals: a pledge or agreement with obligations
- Between God and man: a relationship made by ritual; accompanied by signs, sacrifices, and a solemn oath; sealed by promises of blessing for keeping the covenant and curses for breaking it.[2]

📖 Read Genesis 17:1–4. You will also need to read chapter 16 for context purposes. In chapter 17, we find a third occasion where God tells Abram He wants to be in covenant with him. Why do you think He had to make these promises again? What events are recorded in chapter 16? Why do you think He changed his name?

_____

_____

_____

_____

_____

The whole incident with Hagar illustrates how Abram was still trying to help God fulfill His promises. In effect, God had to keep coming back to say, "Just wait and let Me do it!" Also notice the fact that God kept pursuing Abram. God does not give up on us just because our faith is weak. Over time and with great patience He grows our faith. It may have been to underscore their need of dependence that God changed Abram and Sarai's names and put part of His name (JehovAH) into their names (AbraHAm and SarAH). Name changes were often part of a covenant ceremony. Like many brides today, changing their names to include their husband's name is a covenant sign of connection, commitment, and dependence. God was promising to be "in" them in a way that would enable them to carry out His will and plan for them.[4]

📖 Read Genesis 22:1–18. How many years did it take for Abraham to come to a place of complete trust? (Check 12:4; 16:16; 17:1; 21:34; 23:1 to make a timeline.)

_____

_____

_____

What takes place in chapter 22 is probably about forty years after the initial covenant promises were given. When we realize Abraham endured ten to fifteen years of silence between each revelation from the Lord, we have more sympathy for his doubts and temptations to help bring about the fulfillment of the promises. But here we see Abraham has finally grasped he can wholly trust God to bless him, even if God asks him to sacrifice the son of promise.

📖 Read Matthew 26:26–28, Romans 8:32, Hebrews 2:14–16 and 4:14–16. What type of aid is available to covenant partners? What price was paid to purchase it?

_____

_____

_____

When Christ took the curse for us on the cross, He fulfilled the covenant God made with Abraham and established a covenant with all those who would believe as Abraham did. Every Christian is in covenant with God through Christ. We celebrate a covenant meal each time we partake of the Lord's Supper. Christ not only defeated the devil, He opened the door to

Extra Mile
BLOOD COVENANT

Read Exodus 3:2; 13:21; 19:18; 24:17; and Acts 2:3 to discover what the fire and smoke most likely symbolized. By passing through the pieces without Abram, God was not only promising to be faithful to the covenant, but was also expressing willingness to take the curse if either of them broke it. Clay Trumball in his book, _Blood Covenant_ makes this significant observation:

All the world over, men who were in the covenant of blood-friendship were ready—or were supposed to be ready—to give not only their lives for each other, but even to give, for each other, that which was dearer to them than life itself . . . an Oriental father prizes an only son's life far more than he prizes his own.[5]

heaven and to covenant help. He promises to help us in our time of spiritual need. Our part is to recognize our helplessness without Him. Knowing we are spiritually bankrupt is the first step in finding freedom from our spiritual bondage. It reveals our total inability to generate change within. Just as Abraham and Sarah could do nothing to bring about the promises of God, neither can we. The starting place for us all is at the throne of grace. All He requires of us at this point is faith in His love for us.

APPLY How ready are you to admit you need help?

_____

_____

_____

Do you see yourself in a covenant with God?

_____

_____

What alternate sources of help or escape do you choose instead of going to the throne of grace?

_____

_____

_____

How often do you go to the throne of grace? Do you realize when you don't pray for grace it implies you think you can live without God's help?

_____

_____

_____

How many days/hours/minutes last week did you go without praying?

_____

Why do you think God invites us to "pray without ceasing"? What does that have to do with being in covenant with God?

_____

_____

_____

Did You Know?
TESTAMENT

The word "testament" is another word for covenant. Both in the Old Testament and in the New Testament God reveals to us that He is a covenant keeping God. The Old Testament contains the history of the covenant God made with the people of Israel. The New Testament is the revelation of the covenant Christ establishes with His church. In essence they are one, for all the blood that was shed in the Old Testament was pointing to and made efficacious by Christ's atonement. Both covenants are based on God's amazing love for us.

GIDEON—THE NEED TO LET GO

Poor Hearts
DAY TWO

What we studied yesterday is all fine and good in theory, but when we get down to everyday living and are face to face with our struggles, it is hard to let go of our own devices. Today we will look at the story of Gideon, and hopefully God will show us our need to remove some false dependencies. Sometimes God has to do a lot of pruning to get us to the place of realizing our bankruptcy. Yet, His goal of building our trust in Him and giving us the kingdom can rarely be accomplished by any other means.

Gideon was one of the judges that led the people of Israel after they settled into the Promised Land and before the time of the kings. In Judges 6:12 the angel of the Lord called him a *"mighty man of valor"* even though he was hiding from the Midianites at the time. He was a reluctant leader and insisted that God confirm his call through a series of miracles. (If you want to read that part of the story you will find it in Judges 6.)

Read Judges 7. What do you think is the main point of this story of Gideon? Why did God whittle Gideon's troops down to only three hundred? (See Judges 8:10 to find out how many were in the enemy's camp.) How does this contrast in numbers illustrate poverty of spirit? How does their victory illustrate the kingdom of heaven?

_____

_____

_____

_____

Sometimes God will paint pictures for us to clearly illustrate spiritual realities. He tells us our enemies are the "spiritual forces of wickedness" in Ephesians 6:12. Our efforts to muster any kind of resistance against this daunting enemy without God are foolish and will always end in defeat. Like Gideon we need to allow God to remove anything that would give us a reason to hope apart from Him.

The kingdom of heaven, like the people of Israel, is made up of those who have been freed from the bondage of the oppressors and who maintain freedom by complete trust and obedience to the King of kings. When our King directs us to let go of a false dependency, we would be foolish to hang on to it.

Read Judges 8:22–27. Gideon in his humility refused to be made king and knew only the Lord should rule over the people of Israel. What was his big mistake after that?

_____

_____

_____

Gideon knew he did not have what it takes to be king, but he thought he could hold on to some personal level of spiritual importance by making the jewels of the defeated Ishmaelites into a priestly vestment (ephod) instead of a crown. An ephod was part of the sacred dress of a Hebrew priest. Probably, this lavish garment was a reminder to Gideon of his great victory (even though the victory belonged to God). The ephod turned out to be a snare for him, just as our spiritual victories or ministry endeavors can become snares to us when we focus on our own efforts and forget His grace.

Read 2 Corinthians 9:8–10. What gift does the Lord give to the poor in heart? What are we to do with the gift, and what kind of harvest is reaped when we do it?

ABSOLUTE DEPENDENCE

"We are utterly dependent here, and for my part, I rejoice in this absolute dependence. . . . It is excellent to be weak in self, and better still to be nothing: to be simply the pen in the hand of the Spirit of God, unable to write a single letter upon the tablets of the human heart except the hand of the Holy Spirit shall use us for that purpose. That is really our position, and we should continually cry to the Spirit of God to pour His life into all we do and say."[6]

—CHARLES HADDON SPURGEON

_____
_____
_____
_____

My favorite definition of grace is "the ability God gives to us to obey Him by the power of His Spirit." When all grace abounds to us we have all we need for a harvest of righteousness. We are the poor farmers, and His grace is the seed we sow. We can depend on God to give us what we need to see the changes He wants to make in us. There is nothing in our personal storehouse of righteousness. The good deeds or the changes in attitude we long to see must come from His supply of grace. We are spiritually poverty-stricken and the sooner we acknowledge it, the sooner we can move towards spiritual growth and blessed living.

📖 Read Matthew 19:16–26. Why did Jesus say that it is hard for a rich man to enter God's kingdom? Why did the rich young ruler bolt when Jesus suggested he give away all his wealth?

_____
_____
_____
_____

The more dependent we are on other things, the less likely we will be dependent on God. This is true in our battle against specific sins as well as our hope for our eternal life.

APPLY What extra "troops" do you count on to help you gain victory over your biggest challenges in life?

_____
_____
_____

How do mood altering drugs and alcohol (or any chosen addiction) temporarily affect your attitudes or sense of blessing?

_____
_____
_____

Why are they a dangerous way to try to bring about change in your attitudes?

_____
_____
_____

Why is permanent change the only real victory? Who can accomplish that change in you? What do you need to let go of in order to allow Him to work in you?

"Thanks be to God who gives us the victory through our Lord Jesus Christ."

1 Corinthians 15:57

_____

_____

_____

_____

PETER—THE NEED TO LAY ASIDE PRIDE

Simon was one of the first of Jesus' disciples, and Christ named him Peter the first time they met. Peter was with Jesus throughout His ministry and was in the inner circle of His closest friends. After Christ's death and resurrection Peter became the leader of the early church. Most everyone loves the apostle Peter. He so embodies our impetuous tendencies, and we can relate to his imperfections because they are so much a part of human nature. We often see ourselves in his failed, exuberant attempts at "keeping the faith." Today we will remind ourselves of some incidents in his life and then read what he wrote shortly before his death. Eventually, he learned what I hope we will all learn in this lesson today.

📖 Read Matthew 4:18–20; 14:26–32; 16:21–23. How would you characterize Peter? What do you think he may have been depending on, besides Christ?

_____

_____

_____

The fact that Peter did not hesitate to leave behind his fishing industry and means of financial support indicates he did not have some common dependency issues. However, his independent spirit that relied upon his own strength and ideas often got him into trouble. How many of us struggle with the same tendency? Our American culture emphasizes and encourages such self-confidence. We are trained from early childhood to be independent and proud of ourselves. Many think "accepting charity" is beneath them and degrading. For us, accepting God's grace is a similar challenge to our pride. We would rather do it ourselves with just a little help than to admit we are poverty stricken and totally unable to affect change in our own hearts.

📖 Read Matthew 26:33, 51–53 and 69–75. What does Peter's statement in verse 33 and his action in verse 52 indicate to you about his pride? Why do you think he was so sure of himself?

_____

_____

_____

Peter did not know himself as well as Christ did. We often think more highly of ourselves than we really are. It takes our failures to show us our true nature and our need for Christ.

📖 Read 2 Peter 1:1–11. Where does faith come from according to the first verse? What does God grant to us according to verses 3–7? Why does

Peter call some people blind and shortsighted in verse 9—what do they fail to see? How is the entrance into the kingdom supplied to us (see verse 11)?

_____

_____

_____

Some people make the mistake of taking verses 5–7 out of its context and think Peter is telling us to work hard at adding these behaviors to our lives by our own effort. This interpretation is given even more credence by the New International Version translation (NIV) which uses the word "participate" instead of "partakers" in verse 4, and omits the words supply in verses 5–7. This suggests an understanding of spiritual growth where God gives faith and we add the knowledge, moral excellence, and so forth. But the New American Standard Bible includes more of the literal Greek "bringing in supply in the faith." Our part is the "bringing in" by faith. We offer nothing from our personal accounts. They are bankrupt.

Go back to the text and underline the following words in each of the verses. **Verse 1:** received, **2:** grace, **3:** granted, **4:** granted, **5:** supply, **8:** qualities, **9:** qualities, **10:** His calling, **11:** supplied. (Note—If you are using the New American Standard Bible [NASB], you will notice in verses 8 and 9 that the word *qualities* is in italics. This means that particular word is not found in the Greek manuscripts but was added by translators to help the passage make more sense in English. But since the context [verses 1 through 11] is talking about grants, I would suggest the word "grant" would have been a better choice than "qualities." Instead of adding qualities we have within ourselves, the context actually refers to grants He so graciously supplies to us.) Each of the words you just underlined implies God is giving us what we need. We are poverty stricken. We add nothing. The "practice" mentioned in verse 10, is practice in allowing His grants like faith, perseverance, and love to be a part of our lives. We are partakers of His divine nature; these are not found in our own natures. The only way we can escape corruption is to receive His grants and practice using them day by day.

Peter has come full circle. At first he thought he could conquer the world with a little help from Jesus. Now he sees it's really all about Jesus, and he is only the poor recipient of precious and magnificent grants. God gets all the glory because from start to finish it is His work and His supply. The kingdom of heaven is a gift. Those who realize their poverty and need are open to receiving it. That is why they are blessed.

 Have you come to a place of not only knowing your need, but also having a willingness to accept help?

_____

_____

_____

Although support groups and friends can offer encouragement and accountability, why are they not sufficient for developing lasting internal change?

_____

_____

WHAT GOD HAS GRANTED TO US

"... His divine power has <u>granted</u> to us everything pertaining to life and godliness, through the true knowledge of Him who called us by His own glory and excellence. For by these He has <u>granted</u> to us His precious and magnificent promises, in order that by them you might become <u>partakers</u> of the divine nature, having escaped the corruption that is in the world by lust." (2 Peter 1:3–4)

 *Word Study*
GRANTED

The Greek word translated as "granted" in the NASB in verses 3 and 4 is the word *doreomai*. It is used only three times in the New Testament, twice here and in Mark 15:45. A grant is a gift given for a particular purpose. The person who receives the grant is obligated to use it for the designated purpose.

Why is divine help our only real hope?

_____

_____

_____

Would you rather have the entrance into eternal life abundantly supplied for you or would you prefer working to deserve it? Why?

_____

_____

_____

_____

What kind of relief is there for you in the idea that you don't have to produce any of these grants in and of yourself?

_____

_____

_____

Do any of the changes you would like to see in your life fit into the categories listed in 2 Peter 1? Which ones?

_____

_____

_____

Poor Hearts

DAY FOUR

PAUL—THE NEED TO LAY ASIDE WORKS

Most of us find it very difficult to accept poverty, either materialistic or spiritual. In fact, Jesus said in Matthew 19 that it would be harder for a camel to go through the eye of a needle than for a rich man to enter the kingdom of God. Saul, Paul's name before God changed it, was a man like the rich young ruler Jesus was referring to, but his "riches" were spiritual. His perceived knowledge of Jewish theology and his zeal to defend the Jewish tradition and faith made him think he was "rich in spirit." As you read the familiar story of Saul's conversion, think about what had to happen in his life to strip him of the "riches" he depended on to bring him life.

Read Philippians 3:4–6 and Acts 9:1–4. What does *"confidence in the flesh"* mean? Make a list of all the things that brought Saul confidence before he met Christ.

_____

_____

_____

What are some similar things that make you think you might be able to impress God with your ability to deserve heaven? Maybe you wouldn't go that far, but are there deeds in your life or personality traits that you hope might enable you to make needed changes in your life?

📖 Read Philippians 3:3, 7–9 and Acts 9:5–19. Make another list of all the things God did to Saul to convince him he was poor and needy. What do you think the Lord meant when He said *"I will show him how much he must suffer"*? What was Saul/Paul's conclusion—what value did his own abilities have?

_____

_____

_____

Not all the things God did in Paul's life are listed in these two passages. He was not only blinded and had to be prayed for by one of the men he had been seeking to imprison, but he was also himself imprisoned, beaten, stoned, shipwrecked, and persecuted (see 2 Corinthians 11:24–27). These experiences were all part of his suffering *"the loss of all things."* Some of the difficulties you face right now could be categorized in this way. God may be allowing these hardships in your life to bring you to a place of realizing the things you count on are rubbish compared to knowing Christ.

📖 Read Philippians 3:10–11. In verse 10, what three things does Paul say he wants to know? How would "knowing" them conform us to Christ's death? What do you think that means? What do you think Paul means by his desire to *"attain to the resurrection from the dead"*?

_____

_____

_____

There is a progression in knowing Christ. It begins with a honeymoon period when we experience the initial joys of intimacy with Him. Then there is growth in knowing the power of His Spirit working in and through us in ministry. But often it is in the next phase, of fellowship with His suffering, where our knowledge of Him grows even deeper. All of this growth is taking us to the place of conformity to His death, or to a place where we die to self, and come alive to Him. Like Paul writes in Galatians 2:20, we are crucified with Christ so that Christ can live in us and through us. Resurrection life has both a present reality and a future fulfillment.

📖 Read Galatians 2:16 and 3:2–7. According to these verses why is it necessary to lay aside our works when we are referring to spiritual wealth?

_____

_____

_____

In these verses Paul makes the case that we are not justified by our works nor are we perfected or sanctified by them. We are justified and sanctified by faith in Christ and by the work of the Spirit in us. Think of spiritual wealth in terms of a bank account in heaven. Since we are spiritually bankrupt in and of ourselves, Christ made the deposit for our "savings" account (justification), and the

Word Study
ATTAIN

The word "attain" in verse 11 comes from the Greek *katantao*. *Katantao* is usually translated elsewhere in Scripture as "come to" or "come upon." The choice of the English word "attain" in verse 11 is perhaps not the best because we usually think of the word "attain" as relating to achievement or arrival by effort. The context makes it clear Paul is talking about coming humbly to Christ and entering into all Christ offers—righteousness, faith, power, and suffering. Resurrection from the dead can only be "come upon" by knowing Christ. There is no attaining it apart from Him.

Holy Spirit makes all the deposits in our "checking" account (sanctification). By faith we make withdrawals from both accounts. Our good works are the fruit of those withdrawals but can never be considered part of the deposits—because we are poor in spirit. We have nothing to deposit. However, we can make withdrawals because we are sons of Abraham and must do it daily because we have no spiritual money of our own.

APPLY Why is the attitude of self-sufficiency so dangerous?

_____

_____

_____

Why do you think Christ made Saul blind?

_____

_____

_____

What is the significance of <u>S</u>aul's name being changed to <u>P</u>aul? (To help you remember, think of his movement from <u>S</u>elf-sufficiency to <u>P</u>overty of Spirit.)

_____

_____

_____

What is necessary to move you from your self-sufficiency to being poor in spirit?

_____

_____

_____

How do you make your daily withdrawals from your spiritual bank accounts?

_____

_____

_____

Poor Hearts

DAY FIVE

JESUS—THE NEED TO DEPEND ON THE HOLY SPIRIT

Try to imagine what it was like for Christ before He became a man. John's description of heaven with streets of gold and beauty beyond compare help us to see the richness of His environment there. The little we know of the fellowship of the Trinity gives a hint of the relational wealth of unbounded love. The brief peek God gave to Isaiah of the worship He receives from angels enables us to imagine the honor He laid aside when He came to earth. The description of His power in creation given to us in Genesis 1 and the statement in Colossians 1:16–17: *". . . all things have been created by Him and for Him. . . . And He is before all things and in Him all things hold together"* show us the strength He suppressed when he took on the limitations of humanity. We will explore today why He would trade such wealth and strength for poverty and weakness.

📖 Read Luke 2:7, Matthew 8:20, and Philippians 2:5–11. Why do you think God's plan included Jesus being put in a manger? How would you describe or define the attitude of Christ mentioned in Philippians 2:5? Why should we have a similar attitude?

_____

_____

_____

_____

_____

_____

Mary laid the baby Jesus in a manger, because that was all Father God supplied for her. But the shepherds were able to identify the Messiah because the angels told them He would be in a manger. God chose to reveal His majesty in a baby to the lowliest men, in the lowliest of circumstances. Was it to prove that all may come to Him? He became poorer than the poorest so none could say, "He did not come for me; therefore, I will not come to Him." Having the attitude of spiritual poverty enables us to come, humbles us before Him, and prompts us to worship.

📖 Read Mark 1:8–13. Why would the creator of the universe need angels to minister to Him? Why do you think it was necessary for Jesus to be baptized with the Holy Spirit?

_____

_____

_____

_____

Even though the mystery of how Christ could be both God and man is beyond our comprehension, I do believe His humanity made it necessary for Him to depend upon the Spirit, just as we need to do. In order for Him to experience every temptation in the same way we do, He became as weak and poor as we are (see Hebrews 4:15). He became poor for our sakes that we might become rich in Him (see 2 Corinthians 8:9).

📖 Read Matthew 14:23; Mark 1:35; Luke 5:16, 6:12, 9:28, 22:39–41; John 14:16, 17:9 and 20. Why do you think it was necessary for Jesus to pray? What do you think He prayed about?

_____

_____

_____

_____

Try to imagine what it was like for Christ before He became a man.

Prayer is the ultimate measure of our dependence on God and our desire to fellowship with Him. If we say we love and trust Him, but seldom spend time in prayer we are deceiving ourselves. We are living in our own strength and depending on other things when we are prayerless. Jesus not only came to redeem us from our sins, He came to show us how to live in dependence on God. Just as He taught His disciples to pray, He will teach us to pray.

📖 Read Acts 11:26 and Revelation 2:17. What is the significance of Christ's name being part of our identity as Christians? What do you think it means that the Spirit will give a new name to all who overcome?

_____

_____

_____

_____

_____

Just as Christ depended on His relationships with the Father and the Spirit and their name is One God, our unity and covenant relationship with the Godhead through Christ is sealed in our receiving the name Christian. God changed the names of every character we studied in this chapter, and it reflects the changes He made in each of them. And He will be faithful to change each of us by His Spirit, and we will be given a new name, written on a white stone, that will reflect the changes He will make in us, enabling us to overcome every enemy, and even our own fleshly desires and temptations.

APPLY If Christ could not live and minister to others without the help of the Holy Spirit, what makes you think you can? How much do you depend on Him?

_____

_____

_____

What things do you pray about and what things do you figure are not worth praying about? What does that reveal about your poverty of spirit?

_____

_____

_____

_____

How often do you pray to be filled with the Holy Spirit? If we were truly poor in spirit, wouldn't we need the Spirit of God to fill us every moment of our lives?

_____

_____

_____

_____

Spend some time with the Lord in prayer.

Dear Heavenly Father, I praise You for loving me so much You have made a covenant with me. Thank You for Your promises that never fail. I praise You that Your grace is sufficient for all my needs.

I confess I do not depend on Your grace enough. I depend on my own strength and wisdom. I depend on others as if they were gods. I depend on mood-altering drugs or food to give me a better attitude. I depend on material things to bring satisfaction. Please forgive my pride that thinks I can make it with a little help from these false dependencies, rather than coming to You in realization of my extreme spiritual poverty and deep need of Your grace. I confess I have sometimes thought of the things I do for You and the ministry I do for others as spiritual riches that give me some value in the kingdom. Rather, help me to see them as only the fruit of Your love in my heart.

Lord, I pray You would fill me with Your Holy Spirit. Please give me the time and desire to be much in prayer. Please deliver me from all the distractions and doubts that keep me from Your throne of grace. Thank You for the promise that the kingdom of heaven belongs to the poor in spirit. May Your kingdom come and Your will be done in my life. Renew my heart, O God.

Use the space provided below to write your own personal prayer.

_____

_____

_____

_____

_____

_____

_____

Works Cited

1. W. E. Vine, *Expository Dictionary of New Testament Words* (Old Tappan, NJ: Fleming H. Revell Co., 1960), 4:62.

2. R. Laird Harris, Gleason L. Archer, and Bruce Waltke, eds., *Theological Wordbook of the Old Testament* (Chicago, IL: Moody Press, 1980), Vol. 1, 128.

3. Malcolm Smith of Unconditional Love Ministries. Additional information can be obtained at www.malcolmsmith.org.

4. Ibid.

5. H. Clay Trumbull, *The Blood Covenant* (Kirkwood, MO: Impact Books, 1975).

6. Charles Spurgeon, *What the Holy Spirit Does in a Believer's Life* (Lynnwood, WA: Emerald Books, 1993, original sermon given in 1865), 35.

7. O. Hallesby, *Prayer* (Minneapolis, MN: Augsburg Fortress, 1931, 1994), 18, 26.

Notes

Broken Hearts

"Blessed are those who mourn,
for they will be comforted" (Matthew 5:4)

Learning to mourn was a long and difficult process for Kim. As a child she learned from her parents that crying was unacceptable and expressing emotion was inappropriate. Kim complied and developed a strong, hard exterior. She learned to avoid tears and keep her heart unmoved. But the hard shell began to crack on a trip she took to India. The pretense that life was good no longer worked as she observed the overwhelming poverty and sorrow of the people of that land.

Several years later she and her husband Brian began a journey with infertility, and a personal season of grief ensued. Those of you who have experienced this trial of life and faith know the ups and downs of hope, the preponderance of advice, the humiliation of testing and intervention, and the sometimes insensitive remarks of others. There was great rejoicing when she finally conceived. *Wow!* she thought, *God has finally answered our prayers. We have endured this trial. He has blessed us and now we are happy and so eager to hold this child He has given to us.*

Four months into the pregnancy an ultrasound revealed her longed-for child was developing without a brain and had no chance of survival. Infertility was hard, but harder still was carrying a child that was dying. Kim said, "Knowing that God experienced the death of His only Son and then commanded us to remember it on a regular basis as we repeatedly take part in the Lord's Supper, showed me He knows that searing, wrenching

Kim . . .

. . . learning to mourn

pain of death and separation and doesn't want us to forget it. Times of sorrow are never to be forgotten—they are to be remembered. In my own times of deepest mourning, it was the memory of Christ's death that I clung to with bearish determination."

Little Michael died peacefully soon after his birth. His parents were able to hold him and say their tearful good-byes. His mother relates:

> I knew I needed to grieve well, or the damage done in my heart and soul would be all the worse. I also learned that people grieve differently. I couldn't expect Brian to experience it all in the same way I did. We mourn when things are not the way they should be. Because this is so, there is room for anger in sorrow. It is not uncommon for our pain to pour out in angry thoughts and words. How important it is for us to come to God to mourn so that our anger vents toward Him, sparing others from the damage we can do when we are in pain. I think God expects our anger, even invites us to bring our anger to Him so He can replace it with comfort. Time for grieving has no boundaries in Christ. Our Lord is constantly broken. We only join Him in sorrow for brief moments of our lives. In those times we may know Him most intimately. Christ alone can contain our broken hearts and mend them when they are shattered.

Kim and Brian did go back to the infertility specialists and tried to conceive again, but never became pregnant. She found a measure of healing when she let go of her own efforts to form a family and accepted what she describes as the Lord's invitation to adopt. They are now the happy parents of two beautiful girls from China. Kim reflects, "God had a plan for the formation of our family that I may have never realized if I had not been infertile and had not experienced a mother's love for the child we lost."

Our culture offers many ways to avoid feeling our sorrow or pain. It often teaches us comfort is the avoidance of pain. Jesus is teaching us a better way. It is in the mourning we experience the comfort. God also uses pain and loss to bring about changes in our heart attitudes. He will sometimes give us deep desires and then withhold their fulfillment in order to reorder our priorities. Grieving can change our perspective on life. It can pull us out of indifference and callousness and turn our hearts towards God and others. When we can get past our fear and anger that life is not what we expected and lift our hearts to the One who is in control of all things, He will not only comfort us but will transform our hearts. When our values have been reprioritized by our grief, we become better citizens of the Kingdom of God. John Piper writes,

> No one ever said that they learned their deepest lessons of life, or had their sweetest encounters with God, on the sunny days. People go deep with God when the drought comes. That is the way God designed it.[1]

Word Study
MOURN

Webster's Dictionary defines this word as "to feel or express grief or sorrow." But biblical mourning is the embracing of pain and/or sorrow for the purpose of renewal. It is endurance that knows God is in the process not just the deliverance.

Broken Hearts

DAY ONE

HANNAH—MOURNING FOR WHAT ISN'T

There are many things to cry about on this fallen planet of ours. We are born into a world under a curse and filled with pain and sorrow because of sin and death. Yet, God has created us in His image and put within us strong desires and longings that can be fulfilled by Him even in the midst of our sorrow. We can find pockets of joy in our pursuit of Him and His plan for us. Today we will look at Hannah's story and see how she mourned the lack of children and how God used her mourning to prepare her for His plan.

Hannah was the favorite wife of Elkanah, an Ephraimite who lived in Israel at the time of the Judges. She was the mother of Samuel, who became the last judge before the kings came into power. She was a woman who knew how to mourn and to learn from her mourning.

📖 Read 1 Samuel 1:1–18. How did God use Hannah's deep sorrow to bring her to the place of complete surrender to His plan? What implications of surrender do you see in these verses? What do you suppose it would take to give a son to the Lord *"all the days of his life"*? Do you think she could have done that had grief not completed the work in her that needed to be accomplished?

_____

_____

_____

_____

I have to wonder if giving her son to the Lord was her idea or His. It seems to me God must have prepared both Hannah and Eli for this strange arrangement that was part of His plan for raising Samuel to be His special servant. Her faith and surrender are also revealed by the change of her countenance after Eli told her to go in peace. Something obviously happened in her heart as a result of her prayer and Eli's words of hope.

Also, did you notice in verse 5 that it was the Lord who had closed her womb? Yet, in verse 15 she pours her soul out before Him. She did not allow anger and bitterness to build a wall between her and the Lord, but surrendered herself and the hope of a son totally to Him. Likewise, when we allow our grief to bring us to a place of surrender, God moves in our behalf to accomplish wonderful things in our lives.

📖 Read Isaiah 30:18. Why do you think God waits to have compassion on us? What significance do you see in the pattern of barren women giving birth to important Bible characters? (See Genesis 18:10–11; 25:21; 30:22–24; and Luke 1:7.)

_____

_____

_____

_____

Imagine how each of these women must have been better mothers as a result of their increased dependency on God, prepared by years of waiting on Him for direction, for wisdom, and for love. Surely, these years of waiting prepared them for nurturing and raising their children to be mighty servants of God. We can learn much in our times of waiting if we go to God for comfort. He waits so we will learn to wait. It is one of the most important lessons for a child of God to learn.

> *"Blessed are the poor in spirit, for theirs is the kingdom of heaven.* **Blessed are those who mourn, for they shall be comforted.** *Blessed are the gentle, for they shall inherit the earth. Blessed are those who hunger and thirst for righteousness, for they shall be satisfied. Blessed are the merciful, for they shall receive mercy. Blessed are the pure in heart, for they shall see God. Blessed are the peacemakers, for they shall be called sons of God. Blessed are those who have been persecuted for the sake of righteousness, for theirs is the kingdom of heaven."*
>
> *Matthew 5:3–10*

📖 Read 1 Samuel 2:1–10, 21. What is the difference between Hannah's first and second prayers? Notice the depth of Hannah's worship in verses 1 through 10. What do you think brought her to that kind of worship? In the end how did the Lord comfort her?

_____

_____

_____

_____

_____

Even though Hannah has just given her young son to Eli, her heart is full of joy. It doesn't seem to come from just having a son, her heart is rejoicing in her Lord. It is her new relationship with the Lord, and her understanding of His ways and His justice that fills her cup. Her focus has changed from herself and her sad lot in life to God—to His holiness, His knowledge, His might, His justice, and His protection.

Larry Crabb has written a helpful book called *Shattered Dreams*. In the parable he uses to introduce his book, he suggests God's purpose in not fulfilling our dreams is to teach us to learn to worship. Although he does not refer to Hannah, her story illustrates his point quite well. The struggle she endured led to amazing worship.

It is true in my own life, when things seem to be going well and I am feeling happy, my worship is often shallow. When God allows circumstances that cause my heart to mourn, my worship is taken to a far deeper level. Crabb writes of a "wonderful dream" of intimacy with God through Christ. Knowing God and enjoying Him fulfills our deepest longings and releases an unsurpassed joy in worship. Could this, at least in part, explain how mourning changes our hearts? Crabb continues:

> The richest hope permits the deepest suffering, which releases the strongest power, which then produces the greatest joy. . . No matter what happens in life, a wonderful dream is available, always, that if pursued will generate an unfamiliar, radically new internal experience. That experience, strange at first, will eventually be recognized as joy.[2]

📖 Read Psalm 40:1–3. How did David's experience parallel Hannah's?

_____

_____

_____

_____

The rock the Lord set Hannah's feet upon was the rock of His sovereignty in her life. Her story and her prayers make it clear that God is in control and will accomplish all of His holy will in our lives. Our times of suffering are part of His plan, and He uses them to make us more like Christ and prepare us for heaven.

📖 Read Hebrews 12:1–3. How did Jesus endure his suffering? How are we to endure our disappointments and sorrow? How can we avoid "losing heart"?

When God allows circumstances that cause my heart to mourn, my worship is taken to a far deeper level.

_____
_____
_____
_____
_____

Hannah could easily be part of that great cloud of witnesses of Hebrews 12:1. Sometimes the sin that so easily entangles us is our hopelessness or lack of faith. Jesus fixed His eyes on the joy set before Him—the joy of one day being united with His perfected bride. I believe His eyes were on us, and He calls us to fix our eyes on Him. Like lovers before their wedding day, our hope of being united with Christ gives us endurance. Considering Him, worshipping Him, and loving Him will carry us through whatever disappointment and sorrow we face. Hannah did not have a revelation of Christ, but her second prayer illustrates how she fixed her eyes on God. We do well to follow her example, and will, like her, experience the promised comfort of God.

APPLY List all the unfulfilled expectations you mourn over.

_____
_____
_____

How do you usually deal with the pain that causes you?

_____
_____
_____

What keeps your disappointments from turning into bitterness?

_____
_____
_____

Has anger ever built a wall between you and God?

_____
_____
_____

Are you prone to fix your eyes on your painful circumstances rather than fixing them on Jesus?

_____
_____
_____

On a scale of one to ten, how would you rate the depth of your worship?

1   2   3   4   5   6   7   8   9   10

NAOMI—MOURNING FOR WHAT IS LOST

Paula Rinehart in her book *Strong Women, Soft Hearts* writes, "Some sorrows in life will never go away. You learn to carry them with you in ways that enrich rather than debilitate your life, in ways that make you wise."[3] Paula is right. The purpose of mourning is not to remove the sorrow—it is a process of learning to carry it. If we are wise and will allow God to change our hearts in the midst of our grief we will be enriched. God will sometimes allow the threat of an all consuming loss to stop us in our tracks and turn our thoughts toward Him and our need of Him. He can use the death or loss of a loved one to draw us closer to Him and to reveal new plans He has for our lives. Today we will look at a woman who endured deep grief, learned from those sorrows, and then found great blessing on the other side of her suffering.

📖 Read Ruth 1:1–5, and 20. The name "Naomi" means pleasant, while "Mara" means bitter. Why did she want her name changed? What does that indicate about her heart attitude?

_____

_____

_____

Naomi did not try to hide her sorrow or pretend her losses did not grieve her to the core. I wonder if one reason Ruth was drawn to her was because of her honest transparency. Gerald Sittser is a man who experienced a similar loss to Naomi's. In a terrible automobile accident he lost his mother, his wife, and a young daughter. Years later he wrote an excellent book on grieving, *A Grace Disguised: How the Soul Grows Through Loss*. One particularly poignant statement that helped him move out of denial and face his grief was the following:

> My sister, Diane, told me that the quickest way for anyone to reach the sun and the light of day is not to run west, chasing after the setting sun, but to head east, plunging into the darkness until one comes to the sunrise. I discovered in that moment that I had the power to choose the direction my life would head, even if the only choice open to me, at least initially, was either to run from the loss or to face it as best I could.[4]

📖 Read Ruth 1:14–21. What can we infer from Ruth's statement that she wanted Naomi's God to be her God? What does Ruth's willingness to leave her parents and their gods imply?

_____

_____

_____

Somehow Naomi's deep faith must have been apparent to Ruth. Ruth's desire to share that faith led to separating her from her idols and choosing to depend on God. Remember that Ruth was also grieving the loss of a husband. As we grieve our losses, God gently reveals to us His love and grace, and we can find a deeper joy in worshipping Him.

THOUGHTS ON SUFFERING

Whatever makes us more and more able to enjoy making much of God is a mercy. For there is no greater joy than joy in the greatness of God. And if we must suffer to see this and savor it most deeply, then suffering is a mercy. And Christ's call to take up our cross and join him in the Calvary road is love.[5]

—JOHN PIPER

📖 Read Ruth 1:22 and Jeremiah 6:16. What do you think is the significance of Naomi's decision to return to Israel after so many years of living in Moab? When is "going back" a good idea?

_____

_____

_____

Although Naomi was mourning the loss of her family, she was also on the road to returning to God and to His people. Like her, we must realize our lives are not just about us. Our lives should instead be centered upon worshipping God and magnifying Him. Returning to "the ancient paths" is a term that implies walking in God's revealed will. Naomi was choosing to return to find rest in God's provision for her by walking in obedience and worship. Turning toward God, not away from Him, in the midst of our mourning guarantees the comfort we long for, even though the sorrow may linger.

📖 Read Ruth 2:20–23, 3:1, and 18. What did God use to change Naomi's heart? How does ministry to others often heal our own wounds? Why is our focus so important?

_____

_____

_____

Ministry to her daughter-in-law gave Naomi new purpose. She began to focus on Ruth's needs rather than her own. Just as Naomi found her own needs met as she sought to help Ruth, we can find new life and purpose in ministry to others. If our grief keeps us in isolation and self-focus, our healing will take much longer. As soon as we move out into God's path for us of loving Him and loving others our hearts begin to heal and our focus is changed. Naomi had learned to "wait" on God, and then she taught her daughter-in-law to wait. Teaching what we have learned is a major building block of ministry.

📖 Read 2 Corinthians 1:3–7, and 11. How can we use our sorrows? How are they wasted?

_____

_____

_____

As we reach out to others who are suffering, our own wounds will be healed. When we ask God to help us not to waste our sorrow, He leads us to comfort others with the comfort we have been given. Learning to pray for others is one way God teaches us compassion and how to share both sorrow and comfort. Learning to share the comfort God has given us and the lessons He has taught us prevents the waste of sorrow.

Years before my life fell apart, someone told me I would someday minister to hurting women. I wondered how that could be and what I could possibly say to them. After experiencing God's comfort and training during a time of grief, I remembered the words of this friend and understood that my losses did have purpose—for they prepared me for ministry.

📖 Read Ruth 4:14–17. How were Naomi's needs met? How was she comforted?

_____

_____

_____

Naomi's story illustrates how loss can usher us into a place of ultimate joy if after walking through the valley of sorrow, we use what we have learned to minister to others. By opening her heart to love and care for Ruth, and to show her how to walk in God's ways, Naomi was healed and rewarded by even more love from a treasured grandson (Obed) and a legacy that produced a king.

🛑 APPLY Do you have appropriate places and rituals to help you mourn? What can your church or Bible study group do to create such opportunities?

_____

_____

_____

How and when have your sorrows been wasted?

_____

_____

_____

What kind of comfort have you stored up over the years of suffering? Do you share it freely?

_____

_____

_____

Have you experienced personal healing in the midst of comforting and ministering to others?

_____

_____

_____

Can you say the following Quaker prayer? Sitting with your hands open in your lap say—"What you put in my hand, Lord, I will receive from you." Then turn you palms over and say—"Whatever you take out of my hands, Lord, I will let go."

Broken Hearts

DAY THREE

DAVID—MOURNING OVER SIN

The kind of mourning that affects our hearts most deeply is repentance. True repentance puts into motion the phenomenal chain reaction that includes God's forgiveness and cleansing. First John 1:9 promises, *"if we confess our sins He is faithful and just to forgive us and cleanse us from all unrighteousness."* With a promise like that, why do we hesitate to confess? We say we want to change. We know we want to be cleansed. What keeps us from true confession and genuine mourning about our sin? Even though our hearts want blessing and comfort, we resist repentance and wonder why. Today we will look at one of the stories of King David to see if we can find some answers to our questions.

📖 Read 2 Samuel 12:1–14. Why do you think David didn't catch on to Nathan's story? According to Jeremiah 17:9; Matthew 7:3–5; and 1 John 1:8, how do we deceive ourselves?

_____

_____

_____

_____

_____

Our deceitful hearts enable us to rationalize our sin. It is so much easier to see the sins of others than our own. David was incensed over the sin of the rich man in Nathan's story, but blind to his own. Whether it is pride or self-protection or something else in our human nature, we are all prone to denial of our own sinfulness. There are times when we are not intentionally hiding it—we actually do not see it. We all need friends like Nathan who are willing to confront us about the sins we do not see and help us to repent.

📖 Read Psalm 51:1–17. List all the different words David uses for sin. What is his attitude regarding his sin? What kinds of sins are implied by his requests in verses 10–12? Have you ever taken a moral inventory of your life? What kinds of sin did you identify?

_____

_____

_____

_____

_____

David doesn't even mention his specific sins of adultery and murder, although they are surely included in his confession of transgressions and blood guiltiness. He goes much deeper than the surface sin and deals with his heart. His desire for a clean heart and a willing and steadfast spirit tells us he is aware of his need for inner transformation. His desire to return to teaching (verse 13) and declaring God's praise (verse 15) indicate an awareness of sins of omission as well. Step Four for those in Alcoholics Anonymous is to take a moral inventory. If we as Christians would follow their lead and use David's psalm as a guide, it would bring us into the blessing of mourning. For if we continue in denial of our sin, we will never find the comfort and forgiveness that mourning and confession supply.

📖 Read Isaiah 22:12–13. What are the two responses recorded in these verses that we can have toward our sin, and why do you think we are drawn to the second one?

"Faithful are the wounds of a friend, but deceitful are the kisses of an enemy."

Proverbs 27:6

_____

_____

_____

When our backs are turned to God and our hearts are closed to His love and forgiveness, we naturally reach out for happiness or comfort from another source. As counselor and author, Gerald May points out, "Addictions displace and supplant God's love as the source and object of our deepest true desire."[6] The Lord God calls us to weeping and wailing, but we often choose gaiety, gladness, eating, and drinking instead. Is it because we don't want to mourn? Is it because our faith is too small? Is it too hard to believe He really loves us and will forgive us again and again? Knowing we don't deserve forgiveness, it somehow becomes easier to mask the sadness and feign happiness. We grab for whatever bit of happiness we think we deserve but turn our backs to God's solution of repentance.

📖 Read 2 Corinthians 7:8–11. How do these verses describe true repentance? List the seven attitudes given in verse 11 for those who truly repent and write down an example for each one.

_____

_____

_____

_____

Has anyone ever rejoiced over your being made sorrowful? Paul understood this second beatitude. He knew the joy and blessedness repentance can bring. In this passage, he explains why mourning over sin is something to rejoice over. Here he teaches the Corinthians (and us) about godly sorrow. This passage contains some key words that describe true repentance. Each of us might think of various ways to define and apply these words. My understanding would be something like this. First of all there needs to be _earnestness_ in my repentance—a serious, intentional, passionate desire to do the will of God, to be forgiven and cleansed. The _vindication_ I desire is an eagerness to clear myself, to be free of the sin I hate. The _indignation_ comes from my anger about the loss of dignity my sins bring upon me. My _fear_ is that I would sin again. The _longing_ is for righteousness and cleansing. The _zeal_ is to pursue His grace—the power over sin and the ability to do His will. And the _avenging of wrong_ or readiness to see justice done is my willingness to accept the consequences of my sin and whatever discipline God may, in His love, use to renew my heart.

📖 Read Psalm 119:49–50. How was David comforted?

_____

_____

_____

David was comforted by the word of God. Is that where you turn when you are afflicted, or mourning, or depressed? It is the word that will bring us hope and comfort. His word will revive and renew our hearts.

> "This is my comfort in my affliction, that Thy word has revived me."
>
> Psalm 119:50

APPLY How does our reputation get bound up in our hesitation to repent?

_____

_____

_____

Why do we fight being broken and humbled before Christ and one another?

_____

_____

_____

Think of a time in your life when God brought you to true repentance. How did you experience both the pain and joy of it?

_____

_____

_____

What do you think of the following question posed by Sue Monk Kidd in her book _When the Heart Waits_:

"How did we get the idea that God would supply us on demand, with quick fixes, that God is merely a rescuer and not a midwife?[7]

_____

_____

_____

JEREMIAH—MOURNING OVER THE SIN OF OTHERS

How do you usually respond to the sin of others? Do you get angry and confrontational, or are you more likely to avoid any contact? The example of Jeremiah introduces a third response. Both anger and denial make the situation worse. Godly sorrow will lead to repentance. Mourning over the sin of others helps us to identify with them, to share in the sorrow God feels, and to see the whole situation from God's perspective. It is the best way to avoid the destructive cycles of conflict or withdrawal. When we face sin with honesty and forgiveness we can help each other to repentance. But when we pretend the sin has no effect on us, our denial feeds resentment. Distancing ourselves only prevents healing and restoration. Anger and revenge perpetuate the conflict. Blessed are those who mourn, for they shall be comforted by renewed hearts, renewed relationships, and real forgiveness. Like Jeremiah we need to grieve to get in touch with the reality of sin, the consequences of sin, and God's remedy for sin. As you read the words of Jeremiah, let them become your words, prompting you to enter with him into an experience of mourning over the sins of others.

📖 Read Jeremiah 7:23–29 and Ezekiel 6:9. What were the sins of the people in Jeremiah's day? Why do you think the Lord told Jeremiah to cut off his hair and "take up" a lamentation?

_____

_____

_____

THE COMFORTER

I believe God wanted His people to see His own sorrow and pain over their sin through His asking Jeremiah to reveal it in his actions. As a prophet for the Lord, he not only spoke the words of the Lord, he acted out the feelings of God. We tend to dwell more on God's anger over our sin rather than His sorrow. Both the Ezekiel passage and Christ reveal the weeping heart of God and help us understand why He told Jeremiah to cut his hair, which was a symbol of mourning.

I vividly remember a time of worship when I was singing a chorus of praise to the Redeemer, when God revealed to me His sorrow over someone's rejection of Christ's redemption. I wept this time not for my own loss, for this person had been very close to me, but for Christ's. I believe the Lord allowed me a brief time of sharing His sufferings and there was in that experience of intimacy a strange joy in the midst of tears. I was not alone.

We are prone to allow others to see our anger rather than our pain when we are responding to their sin. At times our tears could be a far more effective expression of truth. When we refuse to mourn, we are left comfortless. If we put on a stoic front and pretend that someone's sin has no effect on us in order to keep the peace, we end up with a false peace. There is no true comfort in either denial or anger, only in mourning.

📖 Read Lamentations 3:1–8. Jeremiah not only experienced God's sorrow, he was also called to experience Israel's affliction. What are some of the consequences of sin listed in this passage? How do we share those consequences?

_____

_____

_____

We all live in a fallen world. The darkness and brokenness aren't necessarily punishment for personal sins but the consequence of sin in general. Much of the affliction we must bear comes to us, as it did to Jeremiah, by virtue of the fact that we live in a land and a time that has turned its back on God. This was dramatically illustrated for me on a visit to Russia in the early 90s. The darkness and brokenness everywhere reflected the atheism that had reigned over the land for so many years. As I passed by the throngs of people, their eyes reflected hopelessness, sorrow, and pain. No one smiled. No one looked into another person's eyes for connection. No one spoke. Everyone just hurried on. The brokenness of the land was evident on their faces.

📖 Read Lamentations 3:19–26. How does Jeremiah deal with his despair? Why can a Christian enter into a type of mourning that people without hope dare not go?

_____

_____

People who have no knowledge of God's faithfulness need pretense, denial, or addictions to experience some level of comfort or escape. But those who know the love of Christ have hope. We can be more honest in our mourning because we know it is temporary—there will be an end to our tears. As Jeremiah says, it is good that we can wait. Waiting is a big part of mourning. There is a blessed mixture of hope, love, sorrow, and comfort that comes from waiting. Our trust in His faithfulness will grow as we wait. Our love and worship are taken to new depths.

📖 Read Jeremiah 8:18–9:1 and 20. Do you see how Jeremiah's lament is a type of prayer? How does mourning fuel our intercession? Why does he ask us to teach each other to lament?

_____

_____

_____

Prayer that is heartfelt takes us from vain repetition into true intercession. When our hearts are engaged, rather than cold and disengaged, we can embrace our own pain, Christ's pain, and even our enemy's pain. Satan knows if he can keep us in a place of anger and bitterness, we cannot pray. But if we allow the Spirit to teach us to mourn and to forgive from our hearts, we will begin to pray even for our enemies. This type of intercession is most difficult and must be learned from more mature Christians. Verse 20 implies it is especially suited for women who have been trained to mourn by hearing and studying the word of God.

📖 Read Jeremiah 31:10–14. How was Jeremiah comforted?

_____

_____

_____

Jeremiah was comforted by hope. He believed the promises of God, and saw a future day when his mourning would be turned into dancing with joy. He was satisfied with the goodness of God. It reminds me of the refrain we often use in the liturgy at our church. The pastor says, "God is good" and the people reply, "All the time!" Then the pastor says, "All the time" and we reply, "God is good!" This is especially encouraging when we are in the midst of suffering and sorrow.

God is good! . . . All the time!

APPLY What specific sins committed by others have affected your life in most significant ways?

_____

_____

_____

Have you not only mourned the consequences, but the sins as well?

_____

_____

_____

Have you moved through the grief to a place of forgiveness?

_____

_____

_____

If you haven't been able to forgive, what would it take to get you there? Do you understand why forgiveness is necessary?

_____

_____

_____

Do you love others enough to confront them with their sin and help them to repentance? (Note: This type of love comes after mourning over their sin and interceding for them.)

_____

_____

_____

Broken Hearts

JESUS WEPT

Recapping what we saw in Day Four, one of the reasons we are called to mourn is to bring us to a place of intercession. Jesus is the Great Intercessor. His birth, life, and death were ultimately acts of intercession, and we are told in Hebrews 7:25 that He now lives to intercede for us at the right hand of God. The verses we will study today will reveal the sorrow Jesus embraced while here on earth and the pain He bore on our behalf. Even though He is now in heaven, I think He still weeps for us. His tears will not cease until all of His people are with Him and their time of suffering has ended.

📖 Read Isaiah 53:3–6. Why was Jesus prophesied to be a man of sorrows? What was the primary cause of His sorrow?

_____

_____

_____

Anyone who sees Mel Gibson's film *The Passion of the Christ* comes away from the viewing with a vivid awareness of the "stripes" by which we are healed. Before seeing the movie I had always minimized that part of Jesus' suffering. It occurs to me that, in a similar way, I minimize the depth of my sin and my extreme need of healing. He carried our sorrow because we are not only too weak to carry it ourselves, but also sometimes don't comprehend it. The pain we inflict on the heart of God by our disobedience is beyond our ability to even imagine. It is our transgressions that pierce His heart and our iniquities that crush Him. When we wander away from Him and turn to our idols, instead of our loving Lord, Jesus weeps.

📖 Read John 11:35 and its context. Why do you think Jesus wept on this occasion?

_____

_____

_____

Verse 35 does not tell us why He wept, it simply states—*"Jesus wept."* The context, however, does give us some clues. It may have been because of his friend's death or even death in general. He had created us to enjoy life, not to endure death, but sin came into this world and brought with it such unbearable sorrow. It may have been compassion for Mary and Martha—perhaps seeing their tears (verse 33) caused Him to weep. Verse 36 records that the Jews present thought it was His love for Lazarus that made Him weep. The confusion and unbelief of all the people (verse 38) may have also been part of it. Whatever the cause, perhaps a combination of all these reasons, the thing I want you to see is that Jesus was *"deeply moved within."* Even though He was about to raise Lazarus from the dead, He mourned. Even though He knows the ultimate plan for our complete restoration, He weeps with us in our present sorrow.

📖 Read Luke 19:41 and its context. Why is Jesus weeping here? How do you suppose the people who saw Him weeping might have felt? What would they have expected Jesus to do after they had given Him such an overwhelming welcome into their city?

_____

_____

_____

_____

_____

Verses 43 and 44 tell us He wept over the impending doom of the city of Jerusalem. The people who were praising Him thought His miraculous power was going to bring peace and prosperity to their city. They expected Jesus to rejoice in their adulation and lead them to victory and freedom from the Romans. I am sure His weeping puzzled them. Later when they realized He was leading them towards prayer, repentance, and a spiritual revolution, rather than a political one, they cried *"Crucify Him"* instead of *"Hosanna."*

📖 Read Hebrews 12:2–3. How did Jesus endure His suffering and sorrow? Where did Jesus look for comfort? How does this set an example for us?

_____

_____

_____

_____

Jesus did two things to endure. He fixed His eyes on *"the joy set before Him"* and He *"despised the shame."* He held on to hope and refused to let shame

> **When we wander away from Him and turn to our idols instead of our loving Lord, Jesus weeps.**

Word Study
SHAME

The Greek word translated *shame* in this verse is *aischune*, and is usually translated ashamed and "signifies subjectively, the confusion of one who is ashamed [or] objectively, the ignominy which is visited on a person by the wicked."[9] Despising shame would signify fighting against the confusion and not allowing the fear of ignominy to keep one from doing what is right. On the other hand, embracing shame effectively shuts down both our minds and our emotions.

immobilize Him. If we embrace shame it has the power to incapacitate us or imprison us in denial. Like Christ, we must despise it, and refuse to allow it to shut us down. In the power of the Holy Spirit and with the promise of forgiveness we can face our shame head on and deal with it. Mourning can be endured if we mix it with hope. Depression is mourning without hope. Denial is hope without mourning. To mourn effectively we need both hope and honesty. Fix your eyes on Jesus and despise anything that shuts you down or leads you into denial. Fix your eyes on Jesus and He will bring you comfort.

APPLY Why do you suppose it is reported that Jesus wept but never that he laughed? (Remember Isaiah 22:12–13.)

_____

_____

_____

Has this study given you new reasons to mourn or enabled you to get in touch with some sorrows you have tried to deny? Explain your new attitude, if you can.

_____

_____

_____

What comfort have you experienced in the midst of mourning?

_____

_____

_____

A Prayer of Confession

Almighty, eternal, most just and gracious God, help me to know that all things are shadows, but You are substance; all things are quicksand, but You are mountain; all things are shifting, but You are anchor; all things are ignorance, but You are wisdom.

You are thrice holy, yet my life and heart abound with apologies not made, repentance not completed, forgiveness not offered, brothers not respected, reputations not defended, peace not pursued, neighbors not loved, Sabbaths not kept, appetites not restrained, parents not honored, spouse not cherished, children not trained, prisoners not visited, strangers not clothed, hungry not fed, providences ignored, envy unchecked, prayers unspoken, fears not conquered, truth not defended, sheep not fed, feet unmoved, tongue unbridled, eyes unguarded, time wasted, talents wasted, treasure wasted.

Lord Jesus, deliver me from these chains, by your grace. Declare me guilty, but pardoned; lost, but saved; wandering, but found; sinning but cleansed. Give me perpetual brokenheartedness; keep me always clinging to Your cross; flood me every moment with descending grace, and I will praise You forever.[10]

Use the space provided below to write your own personal prayer.

_____

_____

_____

_____

_____

_____

_____

_____

_____

Works Cited

1. John Piper, *Don't Waste Your Life* (Wheaton, IL: Crossway Books, 2003), 73.

2. Larry Crabb, *Shattered Dreams* (Colorado Springs, CO: WaterBrook Press, 2001), 45, 54.

3. Paula Rinehart, *Strong Women, Soft Hearts* (Nashville, TN: W Publishing Group, a division of Thomas Nelson, Inc., 2001), 44.

4. Gerald Sittser, *A Grace Disguised* (Grand Rapids, MI: Zondervan Publishing House, 1995), 33.

5. Quotation from John Piper, *Don't Waste Your Life*, page 62. Used by permission of Crossway Books, a ministry of Good News Publishers, Wheaton, IL 60187, wwwgnpcb.org.

6. Gerald G. May, *Addiction and Grace* (San Francisco, CA: Harper & Row, 1988), 30.

7. Sue Monk Kidd, *When the Heart Waits* (San Fransisco: CA: Harper Collins Publishers, 1990), 28.

8. Charles Spurgeon, *What the Holy Spirit Does in a Believer's Life* (Lynnwood WA: Emerald Books, 1993), 55.

9. W. E. Vine, *Expository Dictionary of New Testament Words* (Old Tappan, NJ: Fleming H. Revell Co., 1960), 1:77–78.

10. Used by permission, taken from PCA General Assembly, 2003.

Notes

Kathy Michael	07-356-1156 09-102-83307	timkat2@hotmail.com
Marilyn Liu	07-558-4842	ritzer@mail.nsysu.edu.tw
Nobuko Sugimoto	07-537-5398 09-720-28084	nobuko77@wc4.so-net.ne.jp
Peggy Owen	07-370-8991 09-114-93775	pegowen1@yahoo.com
Rebecca Hsieh	07-363-4999 09-195-08485	rebecca_hsieh@yahoo.com
Ruth Hanson	06-583-7801 ext. 814	hanson741@yahoo.com
Tiffany Multra	07-356-1146	multrat@mca.org.tw
Tracy Tsai	07-398-4703 09-335-67745	No. 34 Ming-Fung Road San Min District, Kaohsiung john601116@yahoo.com.tw
Jeanay Stiles	08-832-8940	djstiles24@yahoo.com

Kaohsiung Women's Bible Study

Name	Phone	Address/Email
Angela Choi	07-356-2518	choiga@shaw.ca
Annie Chou	07-215-9006 09-287-97806	anniechou1@yahoo.com
Ashley Tsai	07-749-0026	
Catherine	07-556-8702 09-373-36449	
Dareni N. Lowe	07-735-6532 09-720-42937	1-31 Dongshang Rd. Niaosong, Kaohsiung lowednd@yahoo.com
Debbie Kilgore	09-291-92656	alankilgore2004@yahoo.com
Doris Leung	07-536-4418 09-37732824	dorisshun@yahoo.com
Enya Huesing	07-335-9763	enyasun@yahoo.com
Jenny Li	07-385-7918 07-389-9818	
Julie Gadbury	07-550-7800 09-631-10997	j_gadbury@hotmail.com

adopted
baby

Alan Kilgore

0920 - 114873

368 - 3087 (o)

361 - 8347 (H)

if no answer
after 6 rings
it transfer to
Dewie's phone

Surrendered Hearts

"Blessed are the meek,
for they shall inherit the earth." (Matthew 5:6)

With all her heart she wanted to bolt but was totally immobilized in a body cast. Nothing was working out the way she wanted. All alone she waited in fear for the last thing a seventeen year old could want. Why didn't God answer her prayers? She knew He could, because He had healed her father miraculously when he was her age. Why was God making her go through yet another excruciatingly painful surgery—one that would keep her in bed for a full year. She could think of a lot better things to do with her life.

As Alona lay in the dark room she realized she had no choice but to go through with the surgery—the spinal fusion had to be done or her scoliosis would shorten her life span.

Looking back she sees that dark night as her Gethsemane. Fear and dread overwhelmed her. She wished "this cup" could pass from her. Could she surrender fully to a sovereign God who refused to give her a miracle? At that point she remembered the words of an old chorus that filled her heart and mind:

God is still on the throne.
And He will remember His own.
Though trials may press us,
And burdens distress us,
He will never leave us alone.

God is still on the throne.
And He will remember His own.
This promise is true.
He will not forget you.
God is still on the throne.[1]

Alona . . .

. . . learning about
meekness

She fell asleep singing the song, and the next day she endured a nine-hour surgery. There were complications, hemorrhaging, and the loss of eleven pints of blood. She didn't come out of the delirium for several days. Her father was by her side when her eyes began to flutter. She seemed to be saying something. Putting his ear to her lips he heard her sing, "God is still on the throne."

Because of that experience, trusting God with her life and future was settled. Psalm 77:19 became very precious to her, "Your path led <u>through</u> the sea, your way <u>through</u> the mighty waters, though Your footprints were not seen." He had taken her through, not around or away from, the mighty waters of affliction. Although she never saw His footprints, she believes the Holy Spirit continued to sing God's promises in her heart throughout the surgery and the long recovery process, sustaining her through the "sea."

Alona learned about meekness that year and has tenaciously held onto the reality that the meek are blessed. She would not trade that important lesson even for a miracle of healing. Many opportunities have been given to her to encourage others when God does not choose to answer prayers in the way they hope He will. She has deep empathy and sensitivity to people in pain, but knows God deals with each of His children in a unique and loving way. Forty years later she looks back on her experience, and comments, "While the cement was still wet, God etched into the fiber of my being a rock solid assurance of His trustworthiness."

The decision made by some translators to retire the word "meek" is regrettable. The modern definition for meekness is weak, mild, and deficient in spirit and courage. Because this is not the scriptural meaning, translators replace meek with words like humble and gentle. Granted, the meek are humble and gentle, but meekness has a far deeper meaning.

Like many words, we can understand meekness more clearly by seeing what it is not. Meekness is not proud, controlling, defensive, resentful, or unapproachable. The meek are able to turn their lives over to God because of their willingness to allow Him to change their hearts: to make them patient, teachable, and submissive.

Surrendered Hearts

DAY ONE

MOSES—"TURNING IT OVER"

Scripture calls Moses the meekest man on earth (see Numbers 12:3). As you read some of the stories about him, notice how careful he was to do everything just as God directed him. Watch, too, for indications of his willingness to "turn" to God and "re-turn" over and over again. We do not turn our lives over to God in one grand moment. "Turning it over" happens moment by moment as we let go of our own designs and independence and go like Moses to the "tent of meeting" to find out what God wants.

📖 Read Numbers 12:1–10. How does this story illustrate Moses' meekness? Was he always that way (see Exodus 2:8–15)? What do you think made Moses meek (see Hebrews 11:24–27)?

_____

_____

When Moses killed the Egyptian he was taking matters into his own hands. This action revealed a heart of pride, impatience, and control. Hebrews tells us he left Egypt by faith, and his faith carried him through forty years of waiting—a time when God was developing perseverance and humility in his heart.

   📖 Read Exodus 33:7–15 and Isaiah 30:1, 2, 9–13, 15, 16. Compare and contrast Moses and the rebellious children of Israel. List the four words found in Isaiah 30:15 that describe meekness. How do they describe Moses?

_____

_____

_____

_____

Moses would go to the tent of meeting regularly to listen to the Lord. He asked Him to teach him His ways and longed for God's favor, presence, and rest. In contrast, the rebellious children of Israel were obstinate and dependent on their own plans and sinful alliances. They looked for other help and were unwilling to listen to God. Wanting to hear pleasant things, they avoided any confrontation by God. They would rather flee on horses than go to a tent of meeting.

Isaiah gives the rebellious people of Israel a recipe for meekness. If they would repent and learn to rest in God's plan and will for them they could be saved from pending disaster. Those with quiet listening hearts like Moses find true strength. Only those who learn to trust God experience the blessing of meekness.

   📖 Read Numbers 20:1–12. What happened the one time Moses was not so meek? What do you think happened to his quiet confidence? What were the consequences? Why do you think they were so severe?

_____

_____

_____

_____

We can all understand what pushed Moses over the edge. His beloved sister had died. There was no water, and the people blamed him. He had enough opposition and grief to cause his temper to flare, and to lose his quiet composure and trusting reliance on God. But when his focus shifted from God to his personal situation and frustration, he spoke to his people in anger and struck the rock rather than speaking meekly to it. His self-centered comment that "<u>we</u> bring you water" (verse 10) was probably seen by God as a lack of treating Him as holy, and his striking the rock as a lack of faith. Jesus' promise that the meek will inherit the land was withheld from Moses, and he could not enter the Promised Land with his people. I wonder if God was teaching us all how important meekness is by this severe punishment of Moses.

"Blessed are the poor in spirit, for theirs is the kingdom of heaven. Blessed are those who mourn, for they shall be comforted. **Blessed are the gentle (meek), for they shall inherit the earth.** *Blessed are those who hunger and thirst for righteousness, for they shall be satisfied. Blessed are the merciful, for they shall receive mercy. Blessed are the pure in heart, for they shall see God. Blessed are the peacemakers, for they shall be called sons of God. Blessed are those who have been persecuted for the sake of righteousness, for theirs is the kingdom of heaven."*

Matthew 5:3–10

FREEDOM TO PURSUE GOD'S WILL

"Think of your sufferings as a weaning from that old sinful habit of always expecting to get your own way. Then you'll be able to live out your days free to pursue what God wants instead of being tyrannized by what you want." (1 Peter 4:2–3)

—THE MESSAGE

What makes meekness so difficult?

_____

_____

Go back to the descriptive words in Isaiah 30:15 and then think of an opposite attitude that may cause you trouble. Draw a line between each of the contrasting attitudes and mark where you think you are on that line. (For example, where do you see yourself on a line between repentance and pride or rest and worry?)

What do you think God is doing in your life today in order to move you closer to meekness?

_____

_____

_____

Surrendered Hearts

RUTH—"COVER ME"

God in His grace wants to give us all we need for life and godliness. But it is only the meek who will accept His gifts. The meek will inherit the earth; they won't buy it. Pride and independence wants to pay its own way, holding us back from accepting what He offers. A lack of meekness deprives us of the abundant life God has promised His children. But those who allow God to renew their hearts to be meek and humble learn to raise their empty hands to heaven and are showered with His blessings. As you read Ruth's story today, look for some of the characteristics of meekness we studied yesterday, and also for a willingness to receive all that the Lord would provide for her.

📖 Read Ruth 1:1–17. How was Ruth different than Orpah? What do you think might be the significance of Naomi's blessing in verse 9? How do you think Ruth knew she could find true rest only by following Naomi and her God?

_____

_____

_____

_____

Orpah kissed, but Ruth clung. Do you see yourself as one who kisses or clings? Do you offer a surface love to Christ that kisses Him on the one hand, but continually goes back to the security of your father's house, to the false idols that bring you comfort, and the hope that one day a husband will come to give you rest. Or do you cling to Christ as your only hope, and willingly follow Him wherever He may take you?

Gregory Mantle wrote the following, "The great sin of man has always been in this direction: a preference of his own will to the will of God; a preference of his own inclinations for God's obligations."[3] God must have changed Ruth's heart from its natural inclination to try to make life work on her own. He alone could have given her the meekness to say what she did to Naomi. For all of us, true rest can only be found in submission to God and His will for us.

📖 Read Ruth 2:2 and 8–12. What do these verses tell us about Ruth's attitude?

_____

_____

_____

Ruth showed her meekness by her willingness to submit, her willingness to work, and her willingness to hope. She asked Naomi for permission to go, meekly accepting the role of a gleaner, and hoping to find favor. Boaz recognized Ruth's willingness in each of these areas, and described it as seeking refuge under God's wings. What a wonderful definition of meekness!

In my own life, I find a willingness to hope is the most difficult. In Ephesians 1:18 Paul prays that the eyes of our hearts might be enlightened so we may know the hope of His calling. "Knowing hope" is a matter for prayer because our blinded hearts often fail to see the hope. If we fail to recognize the hope of God's calling, we have an excuse for inaction. "There is no way I could do that!" we tell ourselves. Eventually, our longings to follow God's call are deadened, leaving us with the illusion of satisfaction and a fruitless life. We go back to the false security of the past, and to our idols. How much better to meekly accept God's calling, knowing His grace will be sufficient? We have hope for the future because He is faithful. He will always supply all we need for life and godliness.

📖 Read Ruth 3:1–9. How difficult do you suppose it was for Ruth to follow these strange directions? According to verse 1, what was Naomi seeking for her? What is the significance of her lying at Boaz' feet and asking him to cover her?

_____

_____

_____

_____

Naomi was seeking security for Ruth. But unlike advice we might hear from today's woman of the world, she does not tell her she must secure her own future by taking control and grabbing all the power she can. Rather, she advises meekness. This is not manipulation or seduction. Naomi knew the laws and ways of God and guides Ruth into resting in His provision. Just as Titus 2:5 gives a mandate to older women to train the younger women to submit to their husbands, Naomi is seen in this passage as training Ruth in the meaning of submission. Submission literally means to "take a position under" in a way that provides covering for the wife and honor for her husband as she affirms his leadership. When Ruth lies at Boaz' feet and asks for his covering, she is symbolically proposing marriage, and offering to be his submissive wife.

Put Yourself in Their Shoes
WHAT WOULD YOU DO?

Imagine you are in Ruth's shoes, which would you be?

- inclined to stay near home
- inclined to stick with your own people
- wanting your comfort and ease
- embracing God's obligation to glean, risk, and follow
- entering the "rest" of submission

📖 Read Ruth 4:13–17 and Matthew 1:5. How was Ruth blessed by her meekness? What did she inherit?

_____

_____

_____

God not only blessed Ruth for her meekness, but He also blessed the world through her obedience. Matthew 1:5 lists her in the line of Christ—as the great-grandmother of David, she is one of the few non-Jewish ancestors of Christ. She inherited the earth because her descendents included Christ and all of those He brings with Him into the new heaven and the new earth. Her "children" will rise up and call her blessed throughout eternity.

🛑 APPLY How difficult is it for you to follow others and take direction from them? What is it in you that wants to call the shots?

_____

_____

_____

_____

Do you see yourself as one who can freely receive the gifts and graciousness of others or do you prefer to make it on your own?

_____

_____

How does submission to a husband teach us about submitting to God?

_____

_____

How does submitting to God enable us to submit to our husbands?

_____

_____

_____

Surrendered Hearts

DAY THREE

> **"Thou madest us for Thyself, and our heart is restless, until it rests in Thee."**
>
> **—St. Augustine**

ESTHER—THE BIGGER PICTURE

Those who are meek recognize that as individuals they are just a small part of a much bigger picture. It is not "all about me." In contrast, an independent spirit leads to a self-centered focus on personal needs. For example, financial advisors tell me I need to build up my retirement account so I won't be penniless in my old age. Obviously, it is good to make wise investments, but ultimately, I need to remember that "the meek" will inherit the earth. It is far more important to have a Kingdom focus, and make our highest priority seeking to establish God's rule in our day-to-day living. He will be sure all our needs are met. A self-centered focus that tries to assure our own security is a foolish choice in the larger scheme of things. Today we are going to look at the story of Esther and see what we can learn from her about meekness.

📖 Read Esther 2:10, 15, and 20. What do you notice about Esther from these verses?

_____

_____

_____

Esther meekly obeyed her uncle Mordecai and took all the advice of Hegai, who was in charge of the harem. Her example is in contrast to Queen Vashti, who we learn in the first chapter of Esther had refused to obey her husband. The queen's refusal to submit was doubly offensive because of her leadership position. Verses 17 and 18 point out her actions would be noted by the rest of the women in Persia and could lead to a women's rebellion.

📖 Read Esther 3 and 4. How does Esther weigh her choices and recognize the bigger picture? What is indicated by her request that everyone fast and pray for her?

_____

_____

_____

_____

Because it could lead to her death Esther was naturally fearful of coming to the king's court unsummoned, but she recognized the truth of Mordecai's words and realized she must attempt an intervention for the sake of her people. However, she did not depend on her own wisdom or strength. She knew she needed God's grace and direction, so she not only prayed and fasted, but asked everyone to join her. Her words at the end of verse 16 clearly illustrate her complete surrender. Don't think of the fasting as a prescription for getting the prayers answered, but rather as a description of the kind of praying which was happening. The intercession was so intense, the ordinary daily necessities were no longer a priority. Her daily needs and desires were trumped by God's Kingdom perspective.

📖 Read Esther 5. Contrast the meekness of Mordecai with the pride of Haman. Why do you think Mordecai refused to bow to Haman? What does that teach us about meekness? (Reread Esther 3:5, 8, and Exodus 20:2–6.)

_____

_____

_____

_____

Haman's pride was fed by Esther's deference but assaulted by Mordecai's refusal to give him honor. Mordecai refused to bow down to Haman because he believed the first commandment prohibited it—You shall have no other gods before Me. His meekness was toward God alone. Mordecai

"Yet, who knows whether you have come to the kingdom for such a time as this?"

Esther 4:14

showed great strength in his resolve to obey God. Not fearing Haman, he was willing to risk civil disobedience and even death.

📕 Read Esther 9:22–32. In what sense did Esther inherit the earth? How was she both blessed and a blessing to many others?

_____

_____

_____

Esther's meekness was rewarded by the destruction of all the enemies of God's covenant people and the celebration of life and liberty. The custom of celebrating Purim is still kept to this day by the Jewish people. The story of Esther is also a prophecy of God's judgment at the end of time. We know God's enemies will be destroyed and God's people will be victorious. The meek will indeed inherit the earth!

APPLY What helps you to gain perspective in order to see the bigger picture?

_____

_____

_____

Do you tend to interpret providence by your circumstances, or the other way around? Why is the grid or perspective that you use to understand life so important?

_____

_____

_____

_____

How often are you driven by your need for security? Would you say security motivates you more or less than your desire to see Christ's kingdom expand?

_____

_____

_____

What examples can you remember of Christ meeting your personal needs while you were focused on His kingdom? What does Matthew 6:33 promise? How does that help you desire meekness?

_____

_____

_____

_____

_____

MARY—"LET IT BE"

Another facet of meekness is to allow God to bring major changes into our lives without fighting for the status quo. So often we find comfort in our ruts and don't want to move on with God's plan. When we turn our lives over to God we need to be ready to go and do whatever He calls us to. When He calls us out of our comfort zones and challenges us to go beyond our own abilities, the meek response is "Yes, Lord!" Some have defined meekness as "strength under authority." It takes real strength to submit. God never forces us to do anything. He is looking for those who, because of their love for Him and trust in Him, are willing to submit to His will for them. He found such a one in Mary, the mother of Jesus.

📖 Read Luke 1:26–38. After she got over her surprise and fear, what was Mary's response to the angel's news? How does her response illustrate meekness?

_____

_____

_____

_____

"Behold, the bondslave of the Lord; be it done to me according to your word." What a perfect illustration of meekness! It reveals the deep humility of voluntary slavery, the surrender to God's plan, and the willingness to be a vessel He can use. Mary didn't ask for time to check with her advisers, or talk it over with her fiancée, or weigh the pros and cons. She simply and meekly accepted God's revelation and call on her life.

> "Behold, the bondslave of the Lord; be it done to me according to your word."
>
> Luke 1:38

📖 Read Luke 1:39–56. How does Mary compare and contrast the meek and the proud in her song magnifying the Lord? If, as most scholars agree, Mary was just a teenager, how do you think she knew all that at such a young age?

_____

_____

_____

_____

Here, Mary introduces many of the concepts we find in the beatitudes. She already knew she was blessed (verse 48), even though her Son had not yet defined blessedness in His sermon on the mount. She knew God regards the humble but scatters the proud. She understood it is the "thoughts of the heart" that define a person. She foresaw God's plan and purpose in overturning humanity's systems of measuring greatness. In her song, she spoke of mercy and hunger in terms of spiritual realities not yet fully revealed. Somehow, she had grasped secrets of God's economy we struggle to believe even on this side of Christ's coming and revelation of truth.

📖 Read John 2:1–11. What can we learn from Mary's admonition to the servants at the wedding? How can a readiness to obey develop true meekness in our hearts?

_____

_____

_____

_____

_____

Even though Jesus had just told Mary that His time had not yet come, she wanted to be ready if and when He did begin to move. If meekness is letting God have His way with us, Mary's words tell us how to be meek, "Whatever He says to you, do it." There is an expectation that the Lord will give direction in His time. We need that same expectation and readiness to obey.

📖 Read Luke 1:42, John 19:27, and Acts 1:7. How was Mary blessed during her lifetime, and throughout the ages?

_____

_____

_____

The passages in John and Acts are the last verses in Scripture that record anything about Mary. They show us the care given to her by both her son and the church. But Elizabeth's prophecy of blessing upon Mary has certainly been fulfilled. Her meekness has been remembered and celebrated by millions.

APPLY How do you respond to change?

_____

_____

_____

Have you ever fought with God about something He wanted you to do, because you were not ready to do it?

_____

_____

What have you learned about the wisdom of letting it be the way He wants it?

_____

_____

_____

_____

Do you find it difficult to submit to God's will? Why?

_____

_____

_____

_____

Jesus—"Not My Will, But Thine Be Done"

Again, Jesus is our perfect example. During His time on earth He showed us what it means to be meek. He had both strength and wisdom and could have chosen to control what He said, where He went, and what He did. But, He chose the way of meekness—to voluntarily put Himself under the authority of His Father, in complete dependence on the Holy Spirit.

📖 Read John 8:28–29; 12:49–50; 14:10. What do these verses teach us about the meekness of Christ? Now read Matthew 10:19–20. How did He instruct His disciples to be meek?

_____

_____

_____

_____

_____

Think about Jesus' claim that He did nothing on His own initiative. What do you think that means? When He said He always did what pleases the Father, our minds can't comprehend the magnitude of His statement. We are so far from the meekness of Christ. Yet, our passage in Matthew 10 clearly states that the same kind of communication and direction is available to us through the work of the Holy Spirit. The goal of a mature Christian should be to have a similar working relationship to that of Christ's with the Trinity. Imagine what that would look like. Jesus said, "The Father abiding in Me does His works." Isn't the Christian life all about the Spirit abiding in us, doing His works?

📖 Read Luke 22:39–46 and John 18:10, 11. What reason for prayer did Jesus give to His disciples? Is that one of your major reasons for prayer? What change occurred in Him from Luke 22:42 to John 18:11? What part did prayer have in that change? If Peter had been praying rather than sleeping, do you think he would have kept his sword in its sheath?

_____

_____

_____

_____

_____

Through prayer, Jesus found God's ways, God's will, God's cup, and God's strength. In contrast Peter, through temptation found his own way and initiative, his own will, his sword, and his sleep. Think about times in your life when things would have turned out differently if you had been more devoted to prayer.

> *"The Father abiding in Me does His works."*
>
> ## John 14:10

📖 Read Matthew 11:29–30. Remember the word translated "gentle" is really "meek." What is the primary lesson we are to learn from Jesus? How does taking His yoke upon us teach us that lesson?

_____

_____

_____

_____

_____

DON'T RUN FROM SUFFERING

"Anyone who intends to come with me has to let me lead. You're not in the driver's seat; I am. Don't run from suffering; embrace it. Follow me and I'll show you how. Self-help is no help at all. Self sacrifice is the way, my way, to finding yourself, your true self." (Matthew 16:24–25)

—*THE MESSAGE*

A yoke is a wooden frame that joins two oxen together so they can work side by side. Jesus is asking us to voluntarily put ourselves into the other side of the yoke He is wearing. Just as He was yoked to His Father, He wants us to be yoked with Him. This is the ultimate picture of meekness. In a yoke we have no control. We can no longer do our own thing. When we take His yoke upon us, we are giving up our right to go our own way.

Paula Rinehart in her book *Strong Women, Soft Hearts* writes,

> Our human tendency in the whole idea of self-denial is to let go of the wrong stuff—repent of the wrong things. Longings, desires, passions, personality—these things are innate, God-given, his idea. They are not the primary stuff of repentance. The real villain is more willful. I will make it happen—my idea, my way, my timing. Self-will always dispenses with trust. And when we won't trust, we take matters into our own hands.[4]

Rinehart's point is a good one. When we turn our lives over to God, we do not give up our good desires or the passions He has put into our hearts. He does not change our basic personality or ask us to be something He has not made us to be. What we are turning over to Him is the control.

📖 Read 1 Peter 2:21–25. What exactly was the example Jesus left us? List each of the five steps listed in verses 21–23 and ask Him to show you how to follow Him in your current suffering. How are you tempted to go in the opposite direction on each step?

_____

_____

_____

_____

_____

_____

I am currently dealing with a difficult relationship and am tempted at each point to differ from Christ. Instead of *committing no sin,* I find resentment in my heart. Instead of *no deceit,* I find myself gossiping about the other person. Instead of *not reviling,* I find myself putting the other person down. Instead of *uttering no threats,* I threaten to end the relationship. Instead of *entrusting myself to God,* I think I have a better plan to follow. I need to die to sin and live to righteousness. I need to repent and turn to my Shepherd who will guard my soul from making some terrible mistakes.

📖 Read Revelation 21:1–7. How will God the Father reward the meekness of His Son?

_____

_____

In the end Jesus will inherit all things, and He promises to share His inheritance with us, His bride. We can't even begin to imagine the glory God will bestow upon Him.

APPLY What would it take for you to be able to hear the Father clearly enough to speak only those words He gave to you? Should that be a goal?

_____

_____

_____

_____

How does prayer keep you from temptation?

_____

_____

_____

Do you see yourself in Christ's yoke? Explain why or why not.

_____

_____

_____

_____

Which one of Christ's steps listed in 1 Peter is most difficult for you to follow? Why?

_____

_____

_____

Extra Mile

THE FATHER'S WILL

Study these additional verses to find more proof of the subordination of Jesus to His Father: Luke 22:29; John 5:36; 10:18; 14:28; 1 Corinthians 11:3 and 15:27–28.

Spend some time with the Lord in prayer.

 Heavenly Father, I praise You for being the sovereign Lord over all. Thank You for giving us so many precious examples of saints who were willing to surrender to Your sovereignty and were blessed in their meekness. Thank You for Your promise that the meek will inherit the earth. I know all things belong to us in Christ.

I confess I am so prone to wanting things my own way, holding on tenaciously to my plans and my desires. Forgive me for being so reluctant to turn things over to You and for living my life often without even thinking about Your will or bringing decisions to You for guidance. I ask you to forgive me for resisting Your yoke and preferring my independence. Help me to see the blessedness of surrender.

I pray for my sisters in Christ who also struggle with surrender. Please help them to realize the security You offer in Your promise of refuge and covering. We are so full of fear and hopelessness. Help us to reckon on Your goodness and grace. Open the eyes of our hearts to know the hope of Your calling.

Lord, I know the enemy feeds me his lies and tries to convince me that my only security is found in personal control. Please deliver me from this evil way of thinking and renew my heart to meekness. I pray this for my own sake as well as for Your glory. I ask that I may be content to say with Christ, *"Not my will, but Thine be done!"*

Write your own prayer in the space provided.

_____

_____

_____

_____

_____

_____

_____

_____

_____

_____

_____

_____

_____

_____

Works Cited

1. Words by Mrs. F. W. Sheffield.

2. W. E. Vine, *Expository Dictionary of New Testament Words* (Old Tappan, NJ: Fleming H. Revell Company, 1966), 3:55.

3. Gregory Mantle, *Beyond Humiliation* (Minneapolis, MN: Bethany House Publishers, 1975), 15.

4. Paula Rinehart, *Strong Women, Soft Hearts* (Nashville, TN: W Publishing Group, a division of Thomas Nelson, 2001), 24.

Notes

Hungry Hearts

"Blessed are those who hunger and thirst for righteousness, for they shall be satisfied" (Matthew 5:6)

Author John Eldridge writes in his book *The Journey of Desire* that there are only three options in life: to be dead, to be addicted, or to be alive and thirsty. He defines deadness as having no desire, no longing, refusing to feel pain.

> Most of the world lives in addiction; most of the church has chosen deadness. The Christian is called to a life of holy longing . . . To live in thirst is to live with an ache. Every addiction comes from the attempt to get rid of the ache.[1]

Deadness! That's how Bethany saw Christianity. That and rules that were impossible to keep. After the heartbreaking deaths of three close friends in less than two years she felt only anger toward God. Enough of death, she would pursue life in whatever form she could find it. Alcohol, drugs, sex—anything to make her feel more alive. Forget the rules. Forget the church. Forget God. She wanted passion, excitement, freedom, and fun. The rebellion and drugs flung her wayward soul into a whirlpool of addiction. An insatiable hunger for love trapped her in destructive relationships with others in the same vortex of rebellion.

Looking for something to do during spring break, Bethany decided to visit her sister in Seattle. She totally overlooked the fact it was Easter week and never imagined that her sister and brother-in-law, who were on staff at their church, would be spending every

Bethany . . .

. . . changing priorities

night at Holy Week services. Although she did not want to, she attended the services with them. Feeling extremely uncomfortable in the church, she was often overwhelmed by tears she didn't understand. At the Saturday night service of repentance, she heard Christians speak honestly about their sin and the grace of God. For the first time she saw Jesus for who He really is and felt Him calling her and breaking her. That night she wrote in her journal, "I need to move to Seattle and go to this church."

Bethany returned to her home in Michigan and continued smoking pot and living with her boyfriend. But now she felt guilty doing it. "What do you think about God?" she asked her boyfriend one day and then added, "I'm going to move to Seattle for God." He was totally baffled and couldn't understand the changes he saw in her.

On a warm summer day, Bethany boarded a plane to return to Seattle. With no money to buy cigarettes or pot, she decided to quit—cold turkey. Amazingly, she experienced no withdrawal symptoms and believed God miraculously delivered her from her addictions. A month later she smoked some marijuana at a concert and was totally disgusted by it. Everything she had loved about it was gone. Since then she has not even been tempted by it.

The first five months of change were an excruciating adjustment period. Commenting on her early frustration, Bethany muses, "It was like watching your twin sister dying. I had to mourn all the losses I was experiencing. Slowly I started choosing differently. You know—God's will over my own. Finally, I let myself die."

At first, Bethany stayed in touch with her boyfriend in Michigan. But after three months she realized she could not continue their relationship. In November, she flew back to Michigan to break up with him. It was not an easy thing to do, but her hunger for righteousness had become stronger than her hunger for their relationship.

Today Bethany still deals with the consequences of her past. As the memories of unconfessed sin continue to surface, she takes each one to the cross, confessing and repenting again. Bethany explains,

> It's like cleaning house. My hunger for righteousness keeps me at it. I want to be totally cleansed. The Holy Spirit is walking me through the process. I am willing to endure whatever pain it takes to make me righteous and to prepare me to help others. I have found my greatest joy comes as I serve others and talk with them about their problems.

Those who are addicted to alcohol or other mood-altering drugs often seek to cover their sorrow, pain, or shame by losing themselves in oblivion. The satisfaction is only temporary, because their problems are still there when they sober up. The gospel offers more—something far more satisfying. But the change and solution to their problems is not easy to come by, for it takes longer. It takes faith. It takes community. It takes a supernatural act of God. But it is available to all those who truly desire it. In this chapter, we will study and discuss five stories from the Bible to illustrate how God causes His people to hunger and thirst for righteousness.

Today Bethany still deals with the consequences of her past. As the memories of unconfessed sin continue to surface, she takes each one to the cross, confessing and repenting again.

Elijah—The Hungry, Thirsty Prophet

James 5:17 tells us Elijah had a human nature just like ours. This speaks not only of hunger and thirst, but of doubt and struggle, of fear and faith, of weakness and a measure of strength. Today we will look at some of the stories of Elijah to understand what Jesus was talking about in this Beatitude, to find out why people who hunger and thirst for righteousness are so blessed.

We are first introduced to Elijah in 1 Kings 17:1, and we learn nothing about him except he was a Tishbite of the settlers of Gilead. James 5:17 gives us some additional information,

> . . . he prayed earnestly that it might not rain; and it did not rain on the earth for three years and six months. And he prayed again, and the sky poured rain, and the earth produced its fruit.

What do you think went through Elijah's mind before he prayed that first prayer? Don't you think he had to grapple with the fact that if it did not rain for three years he would be hungry and thirsty along with the rest of the people?

📖 Read 1 Kings 17:3–6. What do you think God taught Elijah at the brook Cherith?

_____

_____

_____

God often teaches us spiritual truths of provision through our physical experiences. This happened in the early years of Elijah's ministry, as God taught him to trust—the first and most important lesson we all must learn. Elijah was hungry and thirsty for the basic needs of life, but he was also determined to follow God. When we allow our hunger for righteousness to trump all other desires, God not only satisfies our desire for righteousness, but He satisfies our other needs as well. Jesus teaches us in Matthew 6:33, *"Seek first His kingdom and His righteousness, and all these things will be added to you."* Elijah's primary motivation was to obey the Lord. He was learning to rest in God's provision for him.

📖 Now read verses 9–16. How did God teach the widow to hunger for righteousness? What did she have to give up in order to trust and obey?

_____

_____

_____

_____

The widow had to give up the little she had left that gave her the tiniest bit of security. We all hold on tight to those things we think give us security. But if we are to hunger and thirst for righteousness above all else, we need to let go of any vestige of hope that we can provide it for ourselves. Like the widow we must learn to expect God to provide what we need on a daily basis.

"Blessed are the poor in spirit, for theirs is the kingdom of heaven. Blessed are those who mourn, for they shall be comforted. Blessed are the gentle, for they shall inherit the earth. **Blessed are those who hunger and thirst for righteousness, for they shall be satisfied.** *Blessed are the merciful, for they shall receive mercy. Blessed are the pure in heart, for they shall see God. Blessed are the peacemakers, for they shall be called sons of God. Blessed are those who have been persecuted for the sake of righteousness, for theirs is the kingdom of heaven."*

Matthew 5:3–10

"Seek first His kingdom and His righteousness, and all these things will be added to you."

Matthew 6:33

📖 Read 1 Kings 18:1–2 and 17–18. Why do you think God used physical hunger and thirst? How was He dealing with the hearts of His people?

_____

_____

_____

_____

Word Study
RIGHTEOUSNESS

"A gracious gift of God to men whereby all who believe on the Lord Jesus Christ are brought into right relationship with God. This righteousness is unattainable by obedience to any law, or by any merit of man's own, or any other condition than that of faith in Christ. This faith brings the soul into vital union with God in Christ, and inevitably produces righteousness of life, that is, conformity to the will of God."[2]

By making His people experience physical hunger, He exposed their lack of spiritual hunger. The Israelites had allowed their idols to satiate their spiritual hunger. When Ahab tried to blame Elijah for the lack of food and water, Elijah responded, *"I have not troubled Israel, but you and your father's house have, because you have forsaken the commandments of the Lord, and you have followed the Baals"* (1 Kings 18:18). Baal was an idol, and for us it is a symbol of idolatry and addiction. Forsaking the commandments of the Lord is the same as denying our hunger for righteousness. Following the Baals is looking to another source to satisfy whatever hunger we feel.

📖 Read 1 Kings 18:17–39. What do you think Elijah was teaching the people on Mount Carmel? How does his question in verse 21 speak to us?

_____

_____

_____

_____

"How long will you hesitate between two opinions? If the Lord is God, follow Him, but if Baal, follow him."

1 Kings 18:21

Through Elijah God gave His people a huge object lesson. He put His righteousness on the scales with their addictions (idol worship). This is exactly what we need to do whenever we are tempted to turn to our addictions. Print up Elijah's question and post it on your refrigerator, or TV, or front door, or wherever it will serve to remind you that the issue always comes down to a simple choice: what are you really hungry for?

📖 Read 1 Kings 19:1–8. What under the juniper tree got in the way of Elijah's hunger and thirst for righteousness? How did God satisfy Elijah?

_____

_____

_____

_____

This is a beautiful picture of God's tender care and his patient understanding of our frailty. The angel doesn't chide him for his fear or for giving up and wanting to die. He acknowledges that the journey is often too great for us and we need God's supernatural provision to carry on. The important thing is that Elijah came to the Lord with his request. His hunger was in the right direction, even though his request was amiss. God will always satisfy those who hunger for righteousness. We will be blessed even as Elijah was.

 Do you see yourself by the brook Cherith, on Mt. Carmel, under a juniper tree, or on Mr. Horeb? In other words, which desires pull you away from hungering for righteousness: hunger for basic human needs, security, your addictions, or your fears?

_____
_____
_____
_____

Have you ever had an experience like Elijah's on Mt. Carmel? Do you think He is still willing to use His miraculous power to help us overcome our addictions?

_____
_____
_____

Would it help you to think of "kissing Baal" (1 Kings 19:18) every time you are tempted to use your addictive agents? (Think of kissing as a symbol of passionate involvement.) In what ways do your actions relating to your addictive behaviors resemble kissing an idol?

_____
_____
_____

When are you most thirsty for righteousness? What increases your thirst, and what deadens it?

_____
_____
_____
_____

How can we encourage one another? How can we be salt for one another?

_____
_____
_____

Word Study

RIGHTEOUSNESS IN THE OLD TESTAMENT

Before Christ came and offered His righteousness in the place of our own, people understood righteousness to be obedience to the laws and will of God. Forgiveness for failure could be obtained by sacrifices made at the temple.

CISTERN DIGGERS—LOOKING FOR SATISFACTION IN THE WRONG PLACES

Hungry Hearts

DAY TWO

So often our appetites get us into trouble. We hunger and thirst for the wrong things and look for satisfaction in the wrong places. Often we are satisfied with pleasures that fall far short of true joy. Why do we work so hard at digging our own cisterns, when the fountain of life is gushing forth just around the corner? Today we will study what Jeremiah wrote about the "cistern diggers" of Israel to see if he can help us realize what is going on.

Read Jeremiah 2:12–13. According to these verses, what two evils did the children of Israel commit? What do you think the broken cisterns represent?

_____

_____

_____

Word Study
CISTERN

Webster defines a cistern as an artificial reservoir for storing liquids. *The New Bible Dictionary* says it is "a subterranean reservoir for storing water which was collected from rainfall or from a spring. . . . Many cisterns are found in Palestine, where rainfall is scarce from May to September."[3]

The children of Israel forsook the "fountain of living water" to *"hew for themselves cisterns, broken cisterns that can hold no water." "Broken cisterns"* can represent a number of things. One possibility is that the broken cisterns could represent our addictions. Once we realize those cisterns can hold no water and can never truly satisfy our desires, we are ready to forsake them rather than forsaking God. In the Sermon on the Mount, Jesus tells us that those who hunger and thirst for righteousness are truly blessed. He explains through this Beatitude that we will be blissfully happy if we realize our deepest desire is actually for righteousness and not for the counterfeits the world offers. Part of our recovery is to embrace our true longings rather than letting our addictions use up our energy through futile attempts to catch water in broken cisterns.

A second possibility is that the broken cisterns may represent our need to control. The idea of forsaking God to hew our own cistern implies a lack of trust and a desire for independence. If we can create our own supply we do not have to come to the source. When we build our own holding tank, we can convince ourselves we are in control. Such self-reliance may appeal to us, but it's really a form of rebellion.

Read Jeremiah 2:14–18. What do you think the waters of the Nile and the Euphrates might represent? What "rivers" are we seeking to quench our thirst (as an alternative to the Living Water)?

_____

_____

_____

_____

Sometimes when we recognize our broken cisterns are not going to supply a thirst-quenching drink, we look to the rivers our neighbors seem to be enjoying. *If I just had what they had, I would be happy. If I could just land the perfect job, or find the right mate, or see my husband change, or win the lottery, life would begin to work for me and I would finally find the happiness my soul desires.* But again, Jesus and Jeremiah are telling us our satisfaction won't be found in our possessions, our employment, or our marriages. These are all broken cisterns.

Read Jeremiah 2:19–20. What do you think verse 19 means in the statement, *"Your own wickedness will correct you, and your apostasies will reprove you"*? (Apostasy involves turning your back on God.) What do our appetites and longing for easy relief lead us to? How do we use our freedom to serve ourselves rather than for seeking God and His righteousness? Why are we prone to equate freedom with independence?

_____

_____

Because false gods never bring true satisfaction and their worship often leads to dire consequences, we sometimes give up on them without even knowing God's grace and His offer of living water. Millions in Alcoholics Anonymous (AA) have found a measure of freedom by working through "the twelve steps," which are based on the principles of the Beatitudes. But for some in twelve-step recovery programs, even though they have realized their cisterns can hold no water, they still *forsake the Lord, and the 'dread of Him' is not in them."* They choose some other higher power or replace their dependency on alcohol with a dependency on their group, or some other addiction. According to Jeremiah they are still playing the harlot.

Remember there were two evils mentioned in Jeremiah 2:13, and the worst one is forsaking the Lord. Christian freedom is freedom from the bondage of sin. When Christ breaks our yoke of sin and frees us from the bondage to our addictions, He does it to enable us to live for God. He is not giving us freedom so we can be independent, or return to some former lifestyle that was free from problems. He is working for more than recovery. He wants to bring us into a state of utmost bliss in a life lived with God and for God.

📖 Read Jeremiah 3:12–15 and 4:1–2. What steps does Jeremiah outline for those who want to return to the Lord? What promises does he make to them? What part does hungering for righteousness play in all of this?

_____

_____

_____

_____

_____

First we have to acknowledge our iniquity, identify our idols, and admit our disobedience. Then we need to return to God as sons and daughters to acknowledge His lordship over us. He promises to be gracious, and He will not be angry forever. Then He promises to bring us to Zion (a symbol for the place His people live and serve Him) and to give us shepherds to feed us with knowledge and understanding. Obviously, for us this is the church. We also need to put away our detestable things (all our idols and addictions) and not waver. This is where determination, perseverance, dependence on the Holy Spirit and the body of Christ come in.

Finally, Jeremiah says we must swear, *" 'As the Lord lives,' in truth, in justice, and in righteousness."* At first glance this seems to be a strange thing to say. But think about it. Truth, justice, and righteousness are the three deepest longings of every person. And the only way we can find them is through a relationship with the living Lord. If truth, justice, and righteousness become our highest priorities, over and above our personal comfort and idea of happiness, not only will we be satisfied, but also *"the nations will bless themselves in Him, and in Him they will glory."* A pursuit of truth, justice, and righteousness is not only a recipe for personal peace and happiness but it also brings blessing to others.

> *Millions in Alcoholics Anonymous (AA) have found a measure of freedom by working through "the twelve steps," which are based on the principles of the Beatitudes.*

APPLY What are some of your leaking cisterns? How much of your life has been centered around digging them?

_____

_____

_____

_____

_____

What has kept you dependent on your broken cistern?

_____

_____

_____

_____

How would you describe your process of repentance? Where are you in the steps Jeremiah describes in the verses we studied in chapters 3 and 4?

_____

_____

_____

_____

_____

Are you ready to swear, "As the Lord lives" in your pursuit of truth, justice, and righteousness?

Are you ready to swear, "As the Lord lives" in your pursuit of truth, justice, and righteousness? To whom will you swear such an oath? Do you think it would be helpful to have some kind of ceremony surrounding your commitment? Do you think such a promise merely consists of solemn words, or could it represent a totally new lifestyle?

_____

_____

_____

_____

What are you really living for?

_____

_____

_____

_____

THE WOMAN AT THE WELL— "THE DRINK THAT SATISFIES"

Even though marriage was designed by God to be an illustration of His covenant love, it often becomes a false god to those who substitute marital love for His love. Women are especially susceptible to this addiction since security is our primary need. Marriage offers a level of security in a husband's promise to love and care for his wife. But when we factor in the sinful natures of both partners and the unfaithfulness of human love, we are left with many people who are thirsty because of their failed marriages. The woman at the well in our story today is a clear example of someone looking for security.

📖 Read John 4:4–15 and John 7:37–39. What do you think Jesus meant by "living water"? What do you think the *"well of water springing up to eternal life"* has to do with righteousness? How does the Holy Spirit satisfy our thirst for righteousness?

_____

_____

_____

_____

_____

Before dealing with the woman's addictions, Jesus zeroes in on her need. Like her, we are all thirsty people, and the water we find in the wells of this earth never completely satisfy. We are made in the image of God, and in the core of our being we long to be completely like Him. The well of water springing up to eternal life is the work of the Holy Spirit to make us like Christ, to purify and prepare us for eternity with Him. That well, and that well alone, will satisfy our hunger and thirst for righteousness.

📖 Read John 4:16–26. What rivers or wells had this woman tried for satisfaction? Would you agree marriage and religion are often the most common counterfeit sources of righteousness and security? Why do you think that might be true?

_____

_____

_____

_____

_____

The Samaritan woman had tried and failed at marriage five different times. She must have been more tenacious than most of us. Obviously, she thirsted for a relationship that would fill the empty place in her soul. Marriage brings the two parts of the image of God, male and female, together in the embrace of love, so it offers a sense of completion. However, it never fully satisfies, because in our fallen natures the love and reflection of God are not perfect. The heartache the Samaritan woman experienced must have been excruciating—she did not allow the conversation to stay on the subject of marriage but quickly changed it to religion.

Some of us, like her, figure if marriage doesn't work, we'll try religion. If a husband can't satisfy maybe a priest or a prophet can show us the way to fulfillment. We look to man-made forms of worship to bring us to God. When a true leap of faith is too risky, we want a mountain to climb or a meeting to go to so we can find God on our own terms. But Jesus takes fulfillment out of the realm of the natural and explains that worship must be spiritual. We will never find righteousness in our own efforts to do it right, or in religious worship that is not centered in spirit and truth.

📖 Read John 4:27–38. What do you think the "harvest" is? What would it look like to hunger and thirst for righteousness in the lives of others? How would that be accomplished?

_____

_____

_____

Christ's hunger to share the gospel was greater than His physical hunger, and the satisfaction He gained from giving living water to thirsty Samaritans was better than the meal His disciples offered Him. His short discourse on the fields ripe for harvest was meant to whet their appetite for "fruit for eternal life."

📖 Read John 4:39–42. What happened to the Samaritans? How did Jesus change the appetites of the woman at the well and the people of the town?

_____

_____

_____

Jesus was hungry and thirsty to fulfill all righteousness for us.

Jesus was hungry and thirsty to fulfill all righteousness for us. He perfectly obeyed His Father and accomplished the work of salvation. By His perfect life and atoning death He has made the way for us to rejoice together in eternity. The Samaritans in our story came to believe that Christ was indeed the Savior of the world. By faith they accepted His righteousness as their own. They drank of the living water that totally satisfied their spiritual thirst.

APPLY Have you tasted living water? When and how?

_____

_____

_____

In what ways have you been tempted to see marriage as a counterfeit source of happiness and salvation?

_____

_____

_____

How can you tell when religion creeps into your worship?

_____

_____

_____

_____

Have you ever wanted your pastor to be a surrogate source of security for you?

_____

_____

_____

_____

JAMES—OUR PART IN LIVING OUT THE RIGHTEOUSNESS CHRIST GIVES

Can you imagine what it would be like to have Jesus as your older brother? Talk about having to live up to the reputation of an older sibling! You would most likely suffer from a debilitating inferiority complex. Most scholars agree that James, the son of Mary and Joseph and the half brother of Jesus, was the author of the Epistle of James. Who better to bring balance to the church on the topic of righteousness? He had watched the perfect example live a totally righteous life. He had also struggled with faith. As the moderator of the Jerusalem church after Pentecost, he had watched the work of the Holy Spirit in the lives of countless believers. Some had taken Paul's teaching of righteousness by faith alone to mean they could live life any way they pleased and their faith would still save them. James knew that Jesus had not intended for His followers to live with such a cavalier view of sin.

As you read these selected verses from James, you will likely discover the tension in the dual meaning of hungering and thirsting for righteousness. In the previous daily sections for this lesson we have emphasized the truth that righteousness is a gift from God purchased for us by the blood of Christ and received through our faith. James points out true faith will always result in righteous living. The tension comes when we try to understand how righteousness is both a gift and a responsibility. Our finite minds want to choose one truth and discount the other, but Scripture teaches both. So we must believe both realities are true and live in the tension of "now, but not yet." We are *now* made righteous by God in Christ, but we are *not yet* righteous in our day-to-day living and are responsible to hunger for complete righteousness. That hunger will compel us to run to Christ for more of His righteousness and run from the sin that tempts us toward unrighteousness.

Read James 1:1–4. According to James, what is the ultimate purpose for all our trials and testing? How might that be a good definition for righteousness? Do you think James would have us endure for anything less? What does this passage indicate about his own hunger and thirst?

_____

_____

_____

James is hungry to see us *"perfect and complete, lacking in nothing."* But he warns us the journey toward this end is filled with trials and testing. My life and the lives of the people I know and love tell me that "trials and testing" equal pain. Yet, James tells us to consider the pain all joy, because our endurance leads to our perfection. Blessing comes in unexpected ways in Christ's Kingdom, a principle we see over and over again as we study the Beatitudes. I sometimes think how nice it would be if God would just "zap" us to perfection. But instead He uses the process of life in a fallen world to perfect us. Life is not always easy for us to endure, but it does build our faith and dependence on Christ.

Read James 1:17–27. How does James define righteousness in this passage? What things do we need to do in order to obtain righteousness? According to James, if knowing what we do does not make us righteous, in what ways does "true religion" change us?

_____

_____

_____

_____

_____

_____

Righteousness is one of the *"gifts that come down from the Father"* (verse 17). It is the *"righteousness of God"* (verse 20), but is *"achieved"* somehow by us and certainly not by our anger. Verse 21 tells us we *"receive the word implanted"* in humility. But in the next few verses James clarifies that receiving is more than hearing—it involves doing. We haven't really received something we never use. James is not saying our doing makes us righteous; he is saying our receiving must include doing. In verses 26 and 27 he describes the righteous as those who *"bridle their tongues, visit orphans and widows and keep themselves unstained by the world."* If we have truly received the gift of righteousness from God by receiving His word implanted in our hearts, it will cause us to bridle our tongues, to care for others, and to keep ourselves pure. If we never do these things we need to question whether or not the word has been implanted and taken root. Maybe we have never received the gift of righteousness.

Read James 2:14, 26. Is James teaching we are saved by our works, or is he calling into question the authenticity of faith that does not make us hungry and thirsty for righteousness?

_____

_____

_____

Doctrine
SANCTIFICATION

"Sanctification is something that we must pursue, or seek earnestly, if we are to obtain it. While it is God's work we have our part in it; viz.: to make it the object of our earnest desire and pursuit. We attain unto sanctification through presenting our members as servants (literally "slaves") to righteousness and becoming ourselves bondservants unto God."[4]

—R. A. Torrey

_____

_____

_____

_____

_____

Easy-believism is rampant in the church today and has been throughout the history of the church. In 1802 Joseph Alleine wrote a book called *An Alarm to the Unconverted*. In it he warned those who think they are Christians to question their salvation if they are still living a life of disobedience. Hungering and thirsting for righteousness is not an option. However, we also know ultimate satisfaction of complete righteousness will not be ours until we ascend to heaven. Until then we must be patient with ourselves and with others. The struggle against sin must continue; repentance and forgiveness must be a way of life; a continual hunger and thirst must be endured.

📖 Read James 5:7–11. What does James teach us about the blessing and satisfaction we can expect if we are hungering and thirsting for righteousness?

_____

_____

_____

James never doubts that God's compassion and mercy will one day totally satisfy us. But he does remind us that we must have patience and endurance in this life. He implies that the blessing comes only after endurance. This is hard to sell in our culture where the demand is often for immediate satisfaction.

APPLY Do you see yourself as "perfect, complete, lacking in nothing"? If not, are you willing to endure whatever it takes to get you there? What do you think it will take?

_____

_____

_____

Do you doubt your salvation when your life and works don't measure up? In what way do you think such doubt could be a good thing?

_____

_____

_____

Have you ever been tempted to think your eternal security allows you to continue willful sinning? What things in your life give you assurance you have received "the word implanted in humility"? Is your faith the kind that produces good works?

_____

_____

_____

_____

What would you say to someone who claims to be a Christian but does not seem to hunger for righteousness?

_____

_____

_____

_____

JESUS—HUNGERING TO SEE US MADE RIGHTEOUS

Because He was already righteous, Jesus experienced no hunger and thirst for His own righteousness. But He did hunger for us to become righteous—so much so that He was willing to die to make it happen. He so longed to see us made righteous that He was willing to take on our sin in the great exchange. *"God made Him who knew no sin to be sin on our behalf, that we might become the righteousness of God in Him"* (2 Corinthians 5:21). Imagine a hunger so great—one that would compel Him to do such a thing. Today we will study several passages that clearly picture Jesus coming not only to save us from our sin but to make us righteous.

📖 Read Matthew 6:33, Romans 10:1–4, and Philippians 3:9. What is the difference between seeking our own righteousness and seeking His? What do you think it means that the Israelites were *"ignorant of God's righteousness"*? What does it take to *"submit to the righteousness of God"*?

_____

_____

_____

_____

Seeking the righteousness of God is first, and foremost, seeking Christ.

Seeking the righteousness of God is first, and foremost, seeking Christ. The Israelites were ignorant of God's righteousness because they stumbled over the Cornerstone. They did not receive Christ as their promised Messiah, so they could never receive the righteousness He offered. For example, Paul was always hungry and thirsty for righteousness, even before he met Christ. But at first he based his confidence regarding righteousness on his circumcision, his nationality, his obedience to the Law, and his zeal for God. Eventually he recognized all his works were rubbish when compared to the righteousness of Christ. Knowing Christ and being found in Him replaced his former goal of obtaining self-righteousness. But God had to break Paul's pride and show him how poverty stricken he was spiritually before Paul could submit to receiving righteousness as a free gift.

📖 Read 1 Corinthians 1:26–31. According to these verses, how does Jesus *"become to us righteousness"*?

_____

_____

Notice how God-centered the process is. God chooses and calls us; God puts us in Christ; Christ became righteousness for us. Yet all we seem to offer to the process is foolishness, weakness, shame, and baseness. Why must it be that way? Paul indicates it has to do with the fact that no one should boast before God. Unfortunately, our human nature wants to boast. Our entire American culture is built on the dream that we can work hard, be self-sufficient, and find happiness. We think that if we are good enough, we can earn heaven besides. In our pride, we become fools.

📖 Read 2 Corinthians 9:8–10. What needs to happen before a *"harvest of righteousness"* can be reaped? List every word that has "all" in front of it and take a moment to marvel at God's provision.

_____

_____

_____

Think of grace in this context as the ability God gives us to live out His righteousness. First, God makes all grace to abound to us. Next, we receive and acknowledge that His grace is sufficient. Then, we use His abundant grace to do righteous deeds. Finally, verse 10 tells us God causes the seeds we sow to multiply and bring forth a harvest of righteousness. Can you see how it all comes from God, and all the glory must be given to Him. We do have a part, but everything we do is in complete dependence on His grace.

📖 Read Romans 6:5–14. What do we need to do in order to appropriate the righteousness Christ wants to give to us?

_____

_____

_____

Most of what we need to do is mental. We are to *know* we are dead to sin (verse 6). We are to *believe* we are alive with Christ (verse 8). We are to *reckon* we are dead to sin and alive to God (verse 11). The only verb that indicates action on our part is to *present* our members as instruments of righteousness to God (verse 13). Although we have a responsibility to choose, there is passivity implied because we are only the instrument while God is the active one.

Christ longs to make us righteous. Ephesians 5:25–27 tells us He loves us and gave Himself up for us that He might cleanse us and make us holy and blameless. He nourishes and cherishes us because we are members of His body. If we would only truly believe this and submit our lives to His loving direction, we would bear the fruit of His righteousness in us. Righteousness is more about intimacy and surrender than it is about our effort to be like Christ.

APPLY In what ways do you see your hunger for righteousness being satisfied?

_____

_____

_____

What does it mean to you personally that you have been united with Christ in the likeness of His death?

_____

_____

_____

How do you consider yourself to be "dead to sin" and "alive to God"?

_____

_____

_____

_____

Do you enjoy an intimate relationship with Christ?

_____

_____

Have you surrendered yourself as an instrument in His hands?

_____

_____

_____

_____

Spend some time with the Lord in prayer.

Oh perfect Savior, Your righteousness is all I need. My deepest desire is to have my heart renewed in Your likeness. I praise You that this is also Your deepest desire. Thank You for all You have done to make it possible.

Father, I confess my satisfaction with lesser things. I look to food and drink to fill my hunger and thirst. I depend on my addictions to comfort and gratify me. I think my own goodness is sufficient for most circumstances, and I am distracted by the world's offer of material benefits. Too often I expect people to supply the love and affirmation I need. Oh Lord, please forgive me for being such a fool.

I intercede for those I know who are "kissing the Baals" or hoping their broken cisterns will hold enough water to keep them alive. Please use me Lord to testify to the satisfaction I have found in Your righteousness. May I be a light to them that will lead them to the Living Water. Help me to sound an alarm for those who claim they are converted but display none of Your righteousness in their lives.

I pray as Jesus taught us that You would deliver us from evil. I know the enemy is constantly tempting me to turn to other sources for my satisfaction. Please, Lord, deliver me from those temptations. Give me the grace to say "No!"

Works Cited

1. John Eldridge, *Journey of Desire* (Nashville, TN: Thomas Nelson Publishers, 2000), 182.

2. W. E. Vine, *Expository Dictionary of New Testament Words* (Old Tappan, NJ: Fleming H. Revell Company, 1966), 3:298–299.

3. J. C. Whitcomb, *The New Bible Dictionary* (Wm. B. Eerdmans Publishing Co., 1973), 234.

4. R. A. Torrey, *What the Bible Teaches* (Chicago, IL: Fleming H. Revell Co., 1898), 345–346.

5. J. H. Stringer, *The New Bible Dictionary* (Wm. B. Eerdmans Publishing Co., 1973), 491–492.

Notes

Forgiving Hearts

*"Blessed are the merciful,
for they shall receive mercy" (Matthew 5:7)*

*I*f the merciful are truly blessed, why is Min Jung in jail?" That was one of the questions I struggled with on my way to visit a friend who had been arrested. I didn't want to be like Job's friends and come to the conclusion that she must be guilty. There was no doubt she was merciful—I had seen her give mercy to others in so many ways. How could I find out what really happened? Then, clearly in my mind I heard the words, "You are not the judge, just love her!"

I felt nervous and a bit frightened walking into the big county jail complex. It got worse as I had to provide all kinds of information to the man at the desk. If I felt scared, what must it have been like for Min Jung? I was directed to take a seat behind a glass partition in a narrow room where Min Jung and I could see each other and communicate via telephone. Min Jung walked in and burst into tears when she saw me. Actually, I was unable to get much information that first visit. I could only cry with her and assure her that I would be there for her. During my second visit, Min Jung just wanted to talk about all the women she had met there in jail, about their needs, and ways we could work together to help them. Many inmates were sharing their stories and burdens with her because she had developed a reputation as one whose prayers were answered.

It was the third visit before Min Jung was finally able to talk about what had happened. "Kim Wan is young man I know for

Min Jung . . .

. . . mercy that forgives

some time—he have really good interior skills. But he have lots of problems and I try to help him out." In her broken English she went on to explain that she had hired him to rebuild her fireplace. After he finished his work one day he asked to use her computer. She was not feeling well that night, so after setting him up, she took some cold medication and went to bed. The next thing she knew it was 6 a.m. and Kim Wan was yelling "Fire!" She rushed out of her condo to ask a neighbor to call 911. By the time the firemen put out the fire, the police were there, and Kim Wan was gone. They asked her questions about methamphetamines, but she didn't even know what that was. No one believed she had nothing to do with it. Since it was her condo she was responsible, and they took her to jail.

Min Jung spent three months in jail, until Kim Wan was finally apprehended and admitted that she had nothing to do with the attempt to make drugs. When she was released she had nowhere to go. There was nothing left of all her possessions because everything was contaminated and had to be destroyed. The equity she had in the condo was used to pay for the cleanup. A Korean friend told her about a women's shelter for troubled and abused Asian women. It did not take them long to recognize her gift of mercy, and she was asked to be on staff. Although she is still working through the forgiveness process with Kim Wan, she has found much joy and healing in serving others. In some ways, she says, life is simpler there— no worries about bills and buying more things. "I was really, really anger at first—upset with Kim Wan and God. Through the process, even though I lost it, I learned what is the forgiving meaning. Good overcomes evil. Same time, through the prayer, I learned God still loved me."

Mercy has two meanings and Min Jung's story illustrates them both. The first is the willingness to offer forgiveness to one who has offended you. The second is pity or sympathy for the misery of others. In this chapter we will focus more on forgiveness because failure to forgive is such a barrier to true heart change. Min Jung says she has learned, "I must forgive from the bottom of my heart. If part of my heart refuses to forgive, that half keeps coming after me."

Forgiving Hearts

DAY ONE

JOSEPH—MERCY THAT FORGIVES

Joseph was the eleventh son of Jacob and the long awaited first born of Rachel. He was obviously Jacob's favorite and was hated by his brothers because of it. When he was just seventeen he had a dream that his brothers and parents bowed down to him, and naturally the brothers interpreted it to mean that he would some day reign over them. Of course this thought fueled their hate for him even more. Their jealousy eventually led them to plot his death. But Rueben, the oldest son, argued against bloodshed and suggested they throw him into a pit in the wilderness. He intended to rescue him later and bring him back to his father. But before he had the chance, Judah, the fourth son, convinced the other brothers to sell him as a slave to a caravan of Ishmaelites on their way to Egypt. Then they told Jacob that Joseph had been killed and devoured by a wild beast.

Meanwhile, when the slave Joseph arrived in Egypt he was sold to Potiphar, the captain of Pharaoh's bodyguards. Eventually, he became the master of

Potiphar's house then the master of the prisoners when he landed in jail under false charges, and finally he became a magistrate over all of Egypt when his interpretation of Pharoah's dream averted a major famine. We pick up the story when the brothers have come to Egypt for some of the food Joseph had wisely stored up before the famine.

📖 Read Genesis 42:7–20. Why do you think Joseph treated his brothers in this way? What do you think he was trying to accomplish?

to see if they had changed. are they better or worse?

At first we might be tempted to think Joseph was trying to get revenge and make his brothers suffer like he had suffered, but on closer examination I think we see he was looking for repentance. He consistently hid his identity in order to discern what was in their hearts. Their comment about the brother who was "no more" indicated a willingness to speak at least partial truth, but he wanted more.

📖 Read Genesis 42:21–24. What do these verses indicate concerning the brother's repentance and Joseph's response?

Soften heart on both sides

Verse 21 records that they admitted their guilt concerning Joseph to one another and suspected what was happening to them was a punishment from God. Rueben was still doing some blame shifting, and they had not, up to this point, been completely truthful with Joseph. Joseph's tears are interesting in this passage. His heart was obviously tender towards his brothers, and it must have been difficult for him to continue the façade, but he remained steadfast in his attempt to discern the level of his brothers' repentance.

In chapter 44, we see Joseph going even further to see if his brothers are still as self-centered as they were before. He framed the brothers to make it easy for them to sacrifice the youngest to improve their personal standings. Judah then took leadership and full responsibility in refusing to allow Benjamin to stay in Egypt, offering to become the slave in place of his brother. (Remember Judah was the one that originally suggested that they sell Joseph into slavery.) Joseph became completely unhinged by his brother's offer, as Scripture records that he broke down in an emotional display before making himself known to them. Merciful sentiments tugged at Joseph's heart, and he could not continue misleading his brothers any longer.

📖 Read Genesis 45:5–15. What is Joseph's mercy based on? Why do you think he was able to forgive his brothers? What does that teach us about our own relationships?

1) God's love & mercy for us
2) God's revelation of why this happened
3) God knows more about us around has our best (our works) interest. his will
RO 8:28

"Blessed are the poor in spirit, for theirs is the kingdom of heaven. Blessed are those who mourn, for they shall be comforted. Blessed are the gentle, for they shall inherit the earth. Blessed are those who hunger and thirst for righteousness, for they shall be satisfied. **Blessed are the merciful, for they shall receive mercy.** Blessed are the pure in heart, for they shall see God. Blessed are the peacemakers, for they shall be called sons of God. Blessed are those who have been persecuted for the sake of righteousness, for theirs is the kingdom of heaven."

Matthew 5:3–10

Put Yourself in Their Shoes
JOSEPH

If you were Joseph, how would you treat your brothers?

- Get revenge by refusing to give them any food
- Make them feel guilty by shaming them
- Not be concerned with their repentance, only their amends
- Tell them immediately who you are and how angry you are
- Love and forgive them

I haven't seen my siblings in a long time, I'm cautious to reveal too much

Joseph's mercy was based on God's mercy—just as ours must be. We show mercy to others because He has shown mercy to us. Joseph also recognized God's sovereignty and saw how His plan overruled all of the schemes of men. Once we see how *"all things work together for good for those who love God"* (Romans 8:28), we can't stay angry about anything. Bitterness has no place in the heart of a Christian.

📖 Read Genesis 50:14–21. Why do you think Joseph's brothers expected his mercy to end when their father died? What does Joseph's answer to them tell us about him and his mercy?

Satan still held the "fear of death" which what they had.

Joseph had the H.S. and he understood about mercy. He was to teach this lesson.

I don't think Joseph's brothers ever saw the big picture. All this time they thought Joseph forgave them for Jacob's sake. But Joseph knew what we must learn. His question, *"Am I in the place of God?"* implies an important principle of forgiveness. Only God can ultimately judge the hearts of men. When we withhold forgiveness we are taking on the prerogatives of God's justice, deciding their guilt, and meting out the punishment of our disdain. Because we cannot judge, our forgiveness must be unconditional. I think we sometimes hold on to our bitterness because we suspect that God will have mercy on our enemies and we want them to suffer. But we must let God be God. We must trust in His justice and be thankful for His mercy.

must deal with our wounds that caused the need to forgive.

📖 Read Genesis 49:22–26. We have seen how Joseph was merciful. How do these verses describe the blessing he received?

_____

_____

_____

Did you notice that the blessings were both in heaven and here in this life (*the deep that lies beneath*)? Not only did Joseph receive God's mercy, but he also received His strength, His fruitfulness, and His honor. Faith that is coupled with mercy eventually reaps a bountiful harvest.

APPLY Why is forgiving someone the ultimate act of mercy?

Because we give up the right to pronounce judgement on them.

Whom do you need to forgive? *What stops you from forgiving others?*

How does God's sovereignty affect your perspective on forgiveness?

Jesus on the cross, I give over my will to God's sovereignty and I forgive because it's a command!

die to self.

Remember and record an opportunity where you have had to forgive some-one—how did that act of mercy bless you?

it freed me - unforgiveness binds me, it holds me.

THE UNFORGIVING SLAVE— THE DANGER OF WITHHOLDING MERCY

Jesus taught his disciples that human forgiveness was to be uncondi-tional. Because we are not God and cannot see the motives of the heart, or discern our brother's remorse or repentance, we need to forgive no matter what he says or does. This is not just for his sake, but for our own, and for the gospel's sake. When we forgive, our hearts are freed from resentment and bitterness. When we forgive, we are acting out the gospel of God's forgiveness based on what Christ did on the cross. Our forgive-ness is given to others because God has forgiven us, period. There is no excuse for a Christian withholding forgiveness. In fact, Christ tells us that if we choose to withhold mercy from others God will not forgive us! As you read the parable of the unforgiving slave, think about the people who need your mercy.

📖 Read Matthew 18:21–23. Why do you think Peter wanted to limit the number of times he needed to forgive a person? What do you think Jesus meant by *"seventy times seven"*? How is the kingdom of heaven like this parable? How important is forgiveness in the kingdom?

It is our controlling nature that wants to set a specific limit so we can fulfill legalistic requirements. The hyperbole of "seventy times seven" simply indi-cates our forgiveness must be unconditional and never-ending.

Kingdom living requires trust rather than limits. The kingdom Jesus teach-es us about is His rule and reign in our hearts. As we learn to trust His lead-ing, He enables us to forgive. His heart of mercy is implanted in our hearts, and there is no limit to its love and forgiveness. But when we refuse to accept His forgiveness and His reign over us, our hearts remain hard and cold. Just like the servant in Jesus' parable, we have not become a part of the kingdom, even though He has offered us His forgiveness.

☐ Read Matthew 18:24–27. How much was the slave's debt? Do you think the slave had any chance of repaying it in a lifetime? Why do you think the king forgave the slave?

_____

_____

_____

_____

Did You Know?
TEN THOUSAND TALENTS

The *New American Standard Bible* footnotes tell us that ten thousand talents are worth about ten million dollars in silver content though they represent an even larger sum of money in terms of buying power. You have to wonder how a slave could have amassed such debt—but that isn't the point of the parable. On the other hand, the debt owed to the slave by his fellow slave, a denarius, was worth one day's wage, or in our economy, not more than one hundred dollars.

Jesus uses an astronomical figure to represent the debt of our sins. It is such an imposing debt that we have no capability of ever repaying it. Yet, God, in His mercy, because of His own compassion and in response to our request for mercy, grants us forgiveness.

☐ Read Matthew 18:28–30. Why do you think the slave demanded payment from his fellow slave? Do you think he might have intended to use the money to begin paying the king? If so, did he ever truly grasp the fact of his forgiveness? Why would his inability to understand and receive forgiveness be critical?

_____

_____

_____

_____

_____

_____

After finding out about my husband's affair, I read this parable and began making some false applications. I was thinking I had to forgive a huge debt, and saw my own debt as a rather small one. Then the Lord showed me the true meaning of the parable. In James 4:4 we are all convicted of spiritual adultery. I saw how many times I had chosen friendship with the world over intimacy with God. Over the years I had amassed an astronomical debt to God. Comparing my unfaithfulness to God with my husband's unfaithfulness to me was like the slave comparing his debt of ten million dollars to his debtor's meager hundred dollars. The fact that I had been forgiven for my spiritual adultery gave me the grace to forgive my husband's adultery.

Our failure to acknowledge either the size of our debt or the efficacy of God's forgiveness (purchased by the blood of Christ) leaves us with little reason or resource to forgive others. Without the truth of our forgiveness being deeply embedded in our hearts, we are prone to think God expects something from us. This leads us to become stingy and demanding both of ourselves and others. Our greatest need is to comprehend how much we have been forgiven, and then to learn to rest in His mercy. This leads us to become merciful to others and even with ourselves.

☐ Read Matthew 18:31–35. What happened to the unforgiving slave? What might his punishment represent? How does bitterness act as a torturer? What does it mean to forgive from your heart?

_____

_____

_____

_____

_____

I have known many who are enslaved in bitterness. The torture of unforgiveness eats away at their peace of mind and destroys all their relationships. Holding onto resentment produces cold and hardened hearts. Pride results in forfeiting the gift of God's mercy, and arrogance convinces people that they should withhold mercy from others. Forgiveness must come from hearts that have been forgiven. Simply saying the words, "I forgive you" is not enough. Forgiveness is a process that involves honestly dealing with both the causes and consequences of the offence, humility in realizing our own sin, and faith to receive God's grace and enabling to forgive.

📖 Read Luke 6:36–38. What reason for mercy does Jesus give in these verses? What similarities do you find between this passage and the parable in Matthew 18?

_____

_____

_____

_____

_____

In His parable Christ teaches that God's mercy is the origin and source of our forgiveness and our forgiving. Here He teaches that our mercy reflects His mercy. But He expands this thought by explaining how the cycle begun by God's mercy is carried on by us—but can also be broken by us. A beautiful cycle of love, mercy, forgiveness, giving, and blessing awaits us if we choose to live by God's principles of mercy. But if, in our pride, we choose rather to judge, condemn, and withhold our forgiveness, we break the cycle.

📖 Read Colossians 3:12–14. What has God provided for us to help us forgive? How do we put them on?

_____

_____

_____

_____

_____

Paul is not talking about trying hard to be compassionate or kind or humble. Verse one of this chapter tells us to _"seek the things above, where Christ is."_ All of these gifts that are given to us in Christ are to be sought by us. We are to go to Him and ask Him to give us a heart of compassion, kindness, humility, gentleness, patience, perseverance, forgiveness, and love. There is no way we can do it in and of ourselves. To put them on means to receive them and incorporate them into our lives and actions. It takes prayer, and faith, and dependence on Him. The blessing of mercy is ours when we seek it, receive it, and give it.

Why is forgiveness the primary gift of mercy?

_____

_____

_____

When is it most difficult for you to forgive others?

_____

_____

How aware are you of God's forgiveness?

_____

_____

How might unforgiveness be keeping you in bondage to addictions?

_____

_____

_____

Forgiving Hearts

DAY THREE

THE GOOD SAMARITAN—MERCY THAT CARES

Our mercy must extend to those who may not need our forgiveness but still need our love and care. There are many verses in the Bible that make it clear our care for the needy proves we are children of God. But before we can be channels of God's mercy we must realize the mercy He shows to us, as we learned from our study of Jesus' parable yesterday. The two things that prepare us to show mercy are: our realization of the depth of our own sin (and the debt it has incurred) and a realization of the greater depth of God's mercy toward us. Bryan Chapell, president of Covenant Seminary, writes of the connection between the second and fifth Beatitudes:

> My faults are deeper than I care to imagine, but I will never see the need others really have until I dare to consider my own true nature. If I do not consider my own causes for shame, I will judge others instead of loving them. I will distance myself from them instead of recognizing how our mutual needs unite us. I will look down on them instead of embracing them. I will stand aloof, rather than eye to eye. If I stop seeing the person I really am in my mirror, I will stop seeing the faces of others; and then the care that is the vehicle of the Gospel will not flow from me.[3]

Read Luke 10:25–29. How can Jesus say to the lawyer that if he perfectly keeps the Law he will live? What do you think Jesus knows about the Law and the lawyer? Why does the lawyer want to justify himself?

The lawyer can't perfectly keep the law. Jesus knows the law was to point out no ones perfect — the lawyer has trouble loving. #3 who do I HAVE to love to keep the law?

Jesus knows it is impossible for any human (other than Himself) to keep the Law perfectly, but He wants the lawyer to realize that as well. He tells the parable to illustrate how high the bar is and to help the lawyer and those of us who read this passage to recognize our need of another way. We all want to justify ourselves; that is the nature of our sin. But it is our lack of mercy that makes our failure most obvious. We don't love our neighbors as much as we love ourselves. Personally, I know I fail more here than any other place.

📖 Read Luke 10:30–32; Proverbs 14:31, 19:17; and James 2:13–17. How are the poor and needy a test for us?

> *James 2:22 a test? More of an opportunity for mercy to be alone.*

True, active faith meets the needs of the poor. The priest and Levite pass by the man in need and fail the mercy test. When we oppress the poor we bring reproach on God, but when we show mercy we honor Him. Imagine the next time you give to the poor that the gift is a loan to God that He will surely pay back. What better surety could we ask for?

📖 Read Luke 10:33–35; 6:31–38; Romans 12:8; and 1 John 3:16–18. What should be the manner and motive of our mercy?

> *love*

These verses describe the manner of our giving with words like *"liberality,"* *"cheerfulness,"* and *"expecting nothing in return."* Those giving this way have the motivation to be like God, to receive mercy from God, and to abide in His love. Our manner and motive are important because they prove our words and actions stem from the mercy God has planted and is growing in our hearts.

📖 Read Luke 10:36–37 and Matthew 25:34–40. Why does true faith inevitably lead to being merciful?

> *true faith will deny self – then mercy can appear*

We are not made righteous by our good deeds, but our good deeds prove that our faith which is counted as righteousness (see Romans 4:3) is true faith. In Matthew 25 Christ identifies His sheep on the basis of their mercy. The goats thought Jesus was their Lord but their refusal to give mercy to others proved He was not. First God shows us His mercy by revealing His Son, then He gives us mercy by forgiving our sins, and then He enables us to show mercy to others. As Philippians 1:6 says, *"I am confident of this very thing, that He who began a good work in you will perfect it."* This way, God gets all the glory. But we also need to balance this truth with the parallel truth that God also holds us responsible for good works and commands us to show mercy. As Tim Keller points out in his book *Ministries of Mercy,*

Put Yourself in Their Shoes
GIVING SPIRIT

What do you do when you see poor people begging by the side of the road?

- Look the other way to avoid eye contact, and hope the light turns green soon
- Roll down the window and hand him a dollar bill or a tract
- Pray for him, but know that God doesn't want you to get involved
- Offer him a ride to the welfare office
- Sincerely ask God what He wants you to do

We have nothing less than an order from our Lord in the most categorical terms. "Go and do likewise!" Our paradigm is the Samaritan, who risked his safety, destroyed his schedule, and became dirty and bloody through personal involvement with a needy person of another race and social class. Are we as Christians obeying this command personally? Are we as a church obeying this command corporately?[4]

📖 Read Psalm 41:1–3 and Isaiah 58:10–11. What are some other promised blessings that come from being merciful?

deliver in times of trouble, protect & preserve his life, sustain on sickbed & restore from illness. Your light will raise in the darkness & night become like noonday.

I find nine different blessings in these verses. Amazing promises! For those of you in recovery, the fourth one may be especially meaningful. Think about how restoration to health could be exactly what you are aiming for. How does your showing mercy to others bring about your recovery that much sooner? Are you ready for your life to be a watered garden instead of a desert?

APPLY Who are the recipients of your mercy?

_____

_____

_____

What is the scope of your mercy?

how far would I go? my limits are only how far my husband lets me go to.

What is the motive of your mercy?

where comes from the love that Christ lives inside of me. To obey

world view →

When and why do you walk in a wide circle around people in need?

because of my own inadequ- acies, my discomforts.

DAVID—MERCY FOR OUR ENEMIES

Extending mercy to those who almost deserve it is fairly easy, but God's mercy is given to us while we are still sinners (see Romans 5:8). He wants us to reflect His mercy by loving our enemies. This may be the hardest thing He calls us to do. David's example shows us how God enabled him to love King Saul, who was trying to kill him. At one time Saul had loved him greatly, but after David had killed the giant Goliath, became best friends with Saul's son Jonathan, and developed a reputation in the kingdom, Saul became jealous. After several failed attempts to kill David, Saul appointed the young warrior as a commander of all the armies in the hopes that he would be killed in battle. When that didn't work, Saul told his son and all his servants to put David to death. When Jonathan convinced his father to change his mind, things returned to normal for a short time, but soon Saul was throwing spears at David again. Eventually, David had to flee for his life and hide out for years in the wilderness. In chapter 24 we find Saul pursuing him with three thousand men seeking to kill him.

📖 Read 1 Samuel 24. What reason did David give for extending mercy to Saul? What does this indicate about David? How does this help us to think about loving our enemies?

#1 Saul is the anointed of the Lord.
2 David has relationship with the Lord. He honors the Lord David values the relationship with the Lord.
3 my enemy is a child of God too. At one time I was against God.

We see David's respect for God-ordained authority and his deep humility. Respect for others and personal humility are the keys to forgiving our enemies. It is our defensiveness and pride that keep us from it. When we focus on our circumstances and ourselves, we often fail to see the other point of view and God's purposes. We are quick to jump to conclusions that complicate the conflict, like David's men thinking the circumstance was a God-given opportunity to destroy his enemy. David leaves all judgment and retribution in God's hands and seeks only to show his love and respect for his enemy.

📖 Read 1 Samuel 26. Why do you think the whole scenario had to be replayed like this? What indications do you see in this passage that point to David's willingness to wait? What can we learn from the fact that David accepted Saul's apology, though he did not trust him and return with him?

1 It showed God was in this. Before David said for God to decide between them. 2 vs 9-11 David said Saul will die or die in battle. 3 we accept apology + forgive but we are not to ignorant of foolish ways

David again refused to take matters into his own hands. He trusted God to avenge him and was willing to wait for God's timing. I wonder if this was a test of David's resolve. I am sure living in the wilderness was difficult for David, and verse 19 makes it clear lesser men would have turned their backs on a God who made him wait so long. How often are we tempted to seek our comfort and relief from our idols, rather than waiting on God?

It is interesting to note that David did not return with Saul as the king requested according to verse 21 but went on his own way (see verse 25). This tells us it is often necessary to forgive and love from a distance. David for-

PROV 3:35 wise
EPH 5:15 wise

"Love your enemies . . . be merciful, just as your Father is merciful."

Luke 6:35–36

It seems like when mercy is given then repentance the heart is softened and repentance is given a chance.

gave Saul, but he did not trust him. Women in abusive relationships must often separate themselves from the men they love. Forgiving does not mean putting yourself in a place of being hurt again. Forgiveness and reconciliation are two different things. Forgiveness must be unconditional, but reconciliation depends on humility, repentance, and change in the attitudes and spiritual directions of both parties. Even though Saul claimed he had a changed heart, David was wise enough to let time prove the truth.

📖 Read 2 Samuel 16:5–13 and 19:16–23. What can we learn from the way David treated his enemy Shimei?

We see a repentance heart, isn't that what God wants from us?

Years later, after he had become king and reigned for many years, David was forced to flee from Jerusalem because his son Absalom had succeeded in a conspiracy to take power. Shimei was a relative of Saul's and still harbored bitterness against David and used this opportunity to curse him. David again showed amazing resolve to leave his own defense with God and not to strike out against his enemy. Then when he returned to power and Shimei repented, David responded in a way that reflects the mercy of God. Oh, that we would trust in God's sovereignty as David did.

📖 Read Matthew 5:43–45 and Luke 6:31–38. What reason does Christ give us for loving our enemies?

to be son's of our Father in heaven. For the measure you use it will be measured to me.

Our beatitude teaches us that the merciful will obtain mercy. The blessings promised to the merciful are not only for improved relationships in this life but great reward in the life to come. Peace and prosperity experienced on this side of heaven pales in comparison to the blessings stored up for us there. Far beyond our capability of imagining, the joy of sonship will be realized. All of this should give us cause to love and forgive with great abandon.

APPLY Who are your enemies?

_____

_____

_____

What reasons do you have for forgiving them?

peace, love, joy. Blessing here and in heaven.

_____

What barriers do you see that keep you from forgiveness?

_____

_____

What difference do you see between forgiveness and reconciliation in your current difficult relationships?

_____

_____

_____

JESUS—THE MERCIFUL

T he following quote is from B. B. Warfield, a prominent theologian who taught and wrote around the turn of the twentieth century. His comparison of Christ's mercy and our call to mercy makes a perfect introduction to today's study.

Now dear Christians, some of you pray night and day to be branches of the true Vine; you pray to be made all over in the image of Christ. If so, you must be like him in giving . . . "though he was rich, yet for your sakes he became poor" . . . Objection 1. "My money is my own." Answer: Christ might have said, "My blood is my own, my life is my own" . . . then where should we have been? Objection 2. "The poor are undeserving." Answer: Christ might have said, "They are wicked rebels . . . shall I lay down my life for these? I will give to the good angels." But no, he left the ninety-nine, and came after the lost. He gave his blood for the undeserving. Objection 3. "The poor may abuse it." Answer: Christ might have said the same; yea, with far greater truth. Christ knew that thousands would trample his blood under their feet; that most would despise it; that many would make it an excuse for sinning more; yet he gave his own blood. Oh, my dear Christians! If you would be like Christ, give much, give often, give freely, to the vile and poor, the thankless and the undeserving. Christ is glorious and happy and so will you be. It is not your money I want, but your happiness. Remember his own word, "It is more blessed to give than to receive."[5]

As you study Jesus' teaching and example of forgiveness today, be open to comparing His mercy to your own. Let it convict your heart and make you hungry and willing to be more of a conduit of His mercy.

📖 Read Matthew 6:9–15. Why do you think Jesus focused on this one part of the prayer He taught to his disciples? What does His comment indicate about the importance of forgiveness?

forgiveness is essencial to having a relationship with God.

"But if you do not forgive others, then your Father will not forgive your transgressions."

Matthew 6:15

This is one of the hard sayings of Christ. At first it looks like He is teaching that the forgiveness of our sins is based on our forgiving others. We know from other Scriptures that our forgiveness is based on the work of Christ on the cross, and our faith in that work and true repentance in our hearts. So what does He mean? It is helpful to me to think of mercy in terms of our climate cycles. Mercy and forgiveness are flowing from God like rain on the earth. In normal cycles rainwater is collected by rivers and carried to larger bodies of water where it evaporates or continues to flow to larger bodies to evaporate, returning to the clouds—to again rain on the earth. In a lake, such as the Dead Sea, where the water's flow is restricted, the cycles discontinue, and the water becomes salty and unsuitable for normal use. When a Christian refuses to forgive someone, it does not mean she loses her salvation. But she will be unable to receive and experience the flow of mercy in her life. She will not feel forgiven. A closed heart cannot give or receive mercy. Her unforgiveness stops up the cycle.

📖 Read Matthew 7:1–12. Read these verses as Christ's treatise on being merciful. See verses 1 and 12 as brackets that identify His topic of mercy and then ask yourself how each verse helps you to understand how and why we should be merciful. Do you think "the plank" or "log" spoken of in this passage could represent judgmentalism? How does verse 6 balance out verse 8?

Yes. Me giving to people vs God giving to us.

Did You Know?

? MATTHEW 7:1–12

A *chiastic pericope* is a Greek literary form that is similar to the English use of parentheses, where brackets hold a thought together. A *pericope* starts and ends a passage on a topic with a repeated or similar statement. Everything sandwiched between the statements is thereby known to be on that same topic. In Matthew 7:1–12 the *pericope* is bracketed by the similar statements of verses 1 and 12

Notice the "therefore" in verse 12. Remember whenever you see a "therefore" in Scripture, you should ask what it is there for. I think Jesus is tying together His teaching about mercy (see sidebar). Verse 1 and 12 are similar in form—which creates a parenthesis around the verses. I am not suggesting this is the only meaning for each of the verses, but if we look at them in light of our topic of mercy, it will give us new applications. For example, in our mercy we must not judge or focus on the faults of those we are called to minister to. We need to identify our own judgmentalism before we can see clearly to help others. We must ask, seek, and knock for the gift of mercy, depending on the Holy Spirit to guide and enable us to show mercy aright.

Verse 6 offers balance to mercy that has gone too far. Although we are not to judge, this verse calls us to discernment. We are to be giving like our Father gives, and even though verse 8 appears to promise that we can have anything we ask for, we know He does not always give us things just because we ask for them. What we ask for is not always best for us. James 4:3 tells us we sometimes ask with wrong motives. Likewise, we will sometimes need to refrain from giving when it is obvious that our gift will be trampled under foot. It is sometimes a difficult call, and, for those of us who tend to be more tightfisted, it is probably better to err on the side of generosity. Nevertheless, verse 6 serves as an important warning for those rare individuals who may give too much.

📖 Read Mark 14:66–72; John 21:15–17; and 1 Peter 3:9. What do you think Peter learned from Jesus' example of forgiveness?

The completeness of Jesus' forgiveness is made evident in this story. Just as Peter denied Jesus three times, Jesus makes him affirm his love three times. I think the gut-wrenching grief Peter felt in verse 17 was the stab of guilt.

Surely he realized at this point what Jesus was doing and why. We learn from this that our failures do not disqualify us from ministry. But they do keep us humble and mourning. They keep us on the receiving end of God's mercy and call us to the ministry of giving mercy to others. They enable us, like Christ, to give a blessing to those who curse or insult us.

📖 Read Luke 23:34. Who was Jesus forgiving and how is this the ultimate act of forgiveness? What does it teach us about the mercy of Christ?

humanity, His is bigger than mine, I need Jesus to give mercy when I can't.

Dan Allender in his excellent book *Bold Love* says,

> Forgiving love is the inconceivable, unexplainable pursuit of the offender by the offended for the sake of restored relationship with God, self, and others. . . . I will not live with purpose and joy unless I love; I will not be able to love unless I forgive; and I will not forgive unless my hatred is continually melted by the searing truth and grace of the gospel. . . . If love offers life, forgiveness enables love.[6]

APPLY In what areas do you find yourself judging others?

_____

_____

_____

When are you most likely to focus on the faults of others?

when I feel like I'm being judged or condemned.

Have you ever had an experience like Peter's, where conviction of your own failures and forgiveness led to merciful ministry to others?

_____

_____

_____

Do you see yourself in the group Jesus is forgiving on the cross?

Yes.

Close your study time in prayer.

Merciful Father, I can hardly begin to thank You for Your forgiveness. You have treated me like You would Your only Son, although I could never deserve it. Words cannot express the gratitude I feel. But I know the mercy You call me to show to others could begin to express it, so I pray that You would renew my heart to be a heart of mercy.

When I think of all the times I have failed to forgive others, I am bowed down in shame. My heart has been hard, my thoughts full of judgment, and my hands have held tight to all my pride and possessions. Please let the full realization of Your mercy towards me melt my heart, cleanse my mind, and free me to give to others.

I pray that You would teach us to show mercy to one another, to practice mercy here and then take it out to all of those You bring to us. Help us to see You in all the needy ones You bring into our lives. May we experience the blessing of being Your vessels of mercy.

Please deliver me from unforgiveness, from stinginess, from judgmentalism, and hatred of my enemies. I know the accuser of the brethren is constantly feeding my mind with lies about everyone I meet, and all those You have called me to love. Help me to recognize the lies and replace them with Your truth and mercy.

Please help me to sing these words from an old hymn and cause them to fill my heart with mercy:

> Your mercy, my God is the theme of my song,
> The joy of my heart and the boast of my tongue;
> Your free grace alone, from the first to the last,
> Has won my affection and bound my soul fast.
>
> Without Your sweet mercy I could not live here,
> Soon sin would reduce me to utter despair,
> But through Your free goodness my spirits revive
> And He that first made me still keeps me alive.
>
> Your mercy is more than a match for my heart,
> Which wonders to feel its own hardness depart,
> Dissolved by Your goodness, I fall to the ground
> And weep to the praise of the mercy I've found.
>
> Great Father of mercies! Your goodness I own
> And the covenant love of Your crucified Son;
> All praise to the Spirit, whose whisper divine
> Seals mercy and pardon and righteousness mine!

—John Stocker, 1776

Works Cited

1. *Webster's Seventh New Collegiate Dictionary.*

2. J. D. Douglas, *The New Bible Dictionary,* (Wm. B. Eerdmans Publishing Co., 1973), 809

3. Bryan Chapell, *The Wonder of it All* (Wheaton, IL: Crossway Books, 1999), 36.

4. Timothy J. Keller, *Ministries of Mercy* (Phillipsburg, NJ: P & R Publishing, 1997), 11.

5. B. B. Warfield, *The Person and Work of Christ* (Philadelphia, PA: Presbyterian & Reformed, 1950), 574. (I found this quote in both Keller's book on Mercy and John Piper's *Don't Waste Your Life.*)

6. Dan Allender and Tremper Longman III, *Bold Love* (Colorado Springs, CO: Navpress, 1992), 29, 30.

Notes

3/6 to trust more in the Lord with Kandice, Jesse & Sammy.

to ask more of Him about what to do rather than me deciding what to do with my time.

Purified Hearts

*"Blessed are the pure in heart,
for they shall see God" (Matthew 5:8)*

Sarah's heart started closing down early in life. She was the youngest of five children, and no one in the family had much time or affection for her. Her father was mostly absent, and her mother was emotionally unavailable. She tried to make friends, but the negative atmosphere in her home kept her from bringing them there. When she married Ron, things got even worse. Some of his family cut her off. Sarah was rarely included, feeling often their judgment and gossip. Conversations would actually stop when she entered the room, so Sarah spent most of her time in a separate room with her children.

The messages Ron conveyed to Sarah implied that she was weak, incapable, and unintelligent. Even on their honeymoon, he told her she was "pathetic." The power of that word and others like it wounded her deeply. Ron created a dependency in her that crippled her emotionally and spiritually. Although he wanted people to think he was an upstanding Christian man, at home he was totally controlling and abusive. He squelched her personality by constantly pointing out her worthlessness and dismissing her desires. Sarah was living to maintain the façade he created for their family, though her heart was just barely alive and guarded.

Things began to change when she discovered that Ron had a sexual addiction and had for years been in one affair after another. With the help of her church and counselors, she was able to separate from him and begin the process of renewing her heart.

Sarah...

...purified vision

Sarah vividly recalls a point at which she contemplated suicide because the pain and despair had become so oppressive. Through those darkest of days, the Lord spoke clearly to her saying, "I had to break your heart." Somehow the realization that He was using her circumstances to deal with her heart made it all okay. She knew she was safe in the Maker's hands.

Rather than being manipulated and brainwashed by her ~~husband's~~ lies, *Eph 6:12* Sarah could now be the woman God had created. She became focused on the Lord and began to discover who she was and to get in touch with the desires God had put in her heart. She began to rest in the truth that the blood of Christ had purified her heart. Sarah has since found joy and peace in a life of freedom and love. Her loving touch has brought healing and comfort to many who come to her home. Her open hospitality and exuberant joy reveal the person God created her to be.

Sarah knows she did everything she could to save her marriage. Though she is sad that her husband never allowed God to change his heart, she is so thankful that God is changing hers. Although they are still separated, Sarah looks at him differently now. "I have so, so forgiven him. He is no longer my tormentor or a threat to me. I feel a godly love for him, both tender and compassionate. I hope Ron will someday fully repent and allow God to complete His work in him."

Martin Lloyd-Jones gives some background information concerning the Greek word translated *"pure in heart"* in Matthew 5:8: "It is generally agreed that the word has two main meanings. One meaning is without hypocrisy . . . without folds, it is open, nothing hidden . . . sincere . . . single-eyed devotion. The other meaning is cleansed, without defilement."[2] I am intrigued by his phrase "without folds." I believe Sarah's heart had folds or hiding places caused by fear and pain. It was there the love she had to give was hidden away. Finding it difficult to trust or receive love, her relationships were few and shallow. The one love for which she was living turned out to be false, destructive, and untrustworthy. What you love is what you live for, so it affects your desires, passions, affections, and motivations. A purified heart is one that has been cleansed from false loves, one that has been loosed from the destructive love of addictive and false dependencies. A pure heart can love God and others freely, with openness, sincerity, and truth.

Purified Hearts

DAY ONE

SOLOMON—OPEN HEARTS

Solomon was the wisest man who ever lived, and he knew the heart was the most critical part of a man or woman. He was the son of King David and Bathsheba, and at about age 20 became the third king of the nation of Israel. He reigned for forty years. His passion for life is reflected in his writings: most of the Proverbs, the book of Ecclesiastes, and the Song of Solomon. The heart is mentioned over seventy-five times in Proverbs. Today we will study just a few of these occurrences to understand why Solomon emphasized the importance of our hearts, how God begins to purify our hearts, and what kinds of things hamper the purification process.

📖 Read 1 Kings 3:3–15 and Proverbs 8:34. In what ways was Solomon's heart open to God? Why might his openness be important? How does the picture in Psalm 81:10 describe Solomon?

humble himself - servant - little child,
"I do not know", gave honor to father
and to God. 3) a wall or closed off
shuts out. c) hungry & open.

Imagine a baby bird that is all beak with just a bit of flesh at the end of it. He will wait all day with his beak wide open, expecting his mother to come and feed him. This is a picture of a wide-open mouth, ready to be filled by God. Solomon loved the Lord, and his heart longed to worship (a thousand burnt offerings), but he needed wisdom and discernment. (He was still burning incense on the high places—a reference to idolatry.) A literal translation of verse 9 says Solomon asks God for "a hearing heart." Think of ways your own heart could be changed if it were more open to hear what God would say to you.

📖 Read Proverbs 2:1–11. Here Solomon tells us one thing we need to do before our hearts are purified. What is the essence of his message in these verses? How does it compare to Romans 12:2; Ephesians 1:17–18; and 5:26?

ask for it.
accept God's words. B) transform by
the renewing of my mind. ② Pray
for others to have. ③ washing of
water through the word.

A transformed heart begins with a transformed mind. Knowing God and His wisdom leads to a purified heart. Our minds are the original receptacles of His wisdom—we must open them first. But then eventually, as verse 10 tells us, wisdom enters our heart. We need to pray with Paul that God would open "the eyes of our hearts" and that He would cleanse both our minds and our hearts by the washing with His word (Ephesians 5:26). This takes a love of His word, a deep desire to be changed by His word, and a disciplined feeding of our minds through His word. We have to see ourselves like that baby bird, and then let the nourishment He gives us sink down into our open hearts.

📖 Read Proverbs 3:1–6. What instruction about our hearts is given here? What specific things does Solomon tell us to do? How might this give us daily guidance?

Keep commands in hearts. Write
them on my heart, trust in the Lord
with All my heart, B) They are
with us always - we think, act
and love to the measure of what we
believe + know

We are to keep His commands in our hearts, write His kindness and truth on our hearts, and trust Him with all our hearts. We must daily remember His loving plan, His loving presence, and His loving promises. Obedience, faith, and trust come easy when our hearts are open to His love. Hearts filled with His love are blessed by His peace, His favor, and His guidance. Openness must begin anew in our hearts every day. It is not about earning His favor or doing it right—it is opening our hearts to His love.

"Blessed are the poor in spirit, for theirs is the kingdom of heaven. Blessed are those who mourn, for they shall be comforted. Blessed are the gentle, for they shall inherit the earth. Blessed are those who hunger and thirst for righteousness, for they shall be satisfied. Blessed are the merciful, for they shall receive mercy. **Blessed are the pure in heart, for they shall see God.** Blessed are the peacemakers, for they shall be called sons of God. Blessed are those who have been persecuted for the sake of righteousness, for theirs is the kingdom of heaven."

Matthew 5:3–10

📜 **Word Study**
"HEART"

The sixth Beatitude says _"Blessed are the pure in heart"_ (Matthew 5:8).

One of the classic definitions of the word "heart" is the seat of affections. Used in this context our hearts are that mysterious part of us with which we love. Just as our physical hearts pump life-blood to the rest of the body, our spiritual hearts pump love—the life-giving essence that makes life worth living. Because love involves our will, emotions, affections, desires, imagination, conscience, and mind, all of these are components of our hearts. Heart issues like discontent, denial, rebellion, coveting, selfishness, impurity, conflict, and self-protection are the things that keep our lives from true love and deep lasting blessing.

📖 Read Proverbs 4:23. How can we guard or watch over our hearts? What do you think it means that the springs of life flow out of the heart?

_____

_____

_____

_____

Sharon Hersh has written an excellent book called *Brave Hearts,* in which she answers this important question.

> The apostle Paul describes the life of a braveheart: "Go after a life of love as if your life depended on it—because it does" (1 Corinthians 4:1, *The Message*). It's what we were made for . . . women are uniquely designed by God to live and love extravagantly . . . deep within every woman is a heart full of longing for relationships. It is woven into the very fabric of the One in whose image we were made. . . . God created us as the life-givers, the nurturers of relationships; engaging in relationship comes naturally to us. . . . Our design for relationships uniquely reflects God and his wondrous longing to come alongside us, hear our heart's cry, and support us in the storms of life. . . . In order to guard our hearts so they remain free for extravagant love, we must practice discipline, surrender, transparency, and connection.[4]

She goes on to describe the discipline of pursuing God, loving Him with all your heart, and surrendering your heart to Him. The practice of transparency and connection is how we reveal our hearts to others and show our love to them. It takes a conscious effort to understand our own hearts, watch over them, guard them from false love, and free them from anything that would clog the flow of love.

📖 Read Song of Solomon 5:2–6 and Revelation 3:14–20. What do you think it means to open the door of your heart? In what way do you identify with the woman in the Song or the people of Laodicea?

to allow in – to receive – to
accept from others.
I have thought I was in no
need of

Living among sinners who hurt and disappoint us will not only close doors but will also build walls of self-protection. When others wound us, we are tempted to think we are safer to avoid relationships and live independently. Misunderstanding what God is doing in our lives can even close our hearts to Him. The Song of Solomon describes the divine love that is wooing us, the hesitancy we experience in responding to His love, and our confusion when we cannot tangibly experience His presence. The promise given to the church in Laodicea is one of intimacy. Revelation 3 describes the Laodicean church as "lukewarm"; they thought they had everything they needed, and were not open to the passion and purity Christ offers. Satisfaction with our religion, our material wealth, and our empty hearts leaves us without the very thing we were created for. "Buying the gold, garments, and eye salve from Christ is a description of what you do when you open the door of your heart to him." (Don't think of buying in terms of purchasing the free gift of salvation, but rather, of bartering with the affections that keep you satisfied or lukewarm about your faith. Are you willing to give up the lesser loves in your heart to make room for intimacy with Christ?)

📖 Read 1 Kings 11:1–4 and 2 Corinthians 6:11–14. What happened to Solomon's heart? What went wrong? What limitations does God put on our open hearts and why?

_____

_____

_____

_____

I wonder if Paul had Solomon in mind when he warned the Corinthians to limit their "wide-open hearts" to loving and marrying only believers. When we love unbelievers we are naturally drawn to the things they love. Our affections change. Our hearts are pulled in two directions. It is far more difficult to have a heart wholly devoted to the Lord when so much of it is given to loving someone who does not love and serve Him. Solomon held fast to the women he loved and ended up building places for them to serve their idols in order to keep them happy and to keep their love. We must be careful to protect our hearts from dangerous liaisons.

APPLY What things do you see about yourself that indicate your heart is open?

willing to give of myself - serve, love without expecting something in return.

_____

What things threaten your heart? What fears do you have that keep the door closed?

_____

_____

_____

Are you in touch with your deepest desires? What are they?

to be loved

_____

_____

How are you at guarding your heart? Which is hardest for you? The discipline of hearing from God? A daily surrender to His will for you? Transparency to others who will help protect your heart? Or true connections that allow for free flowing love?

_____

_____

_____

Extra Mile

UNEQUALLY YOKED

Read 1 Corinthians 7:12–17 and think how Paul's advice to people who are already married to unbelievers qualifies or modifies the principle of undivided hearts, making it less harsh or restrictive. Keep in mind that in chapter 6 Paul warns single Christians not to marry unbelievers, but here he instructs the pure in heart to find a way to love Christ, their unbelieving husbands, and their children in a way that glorifies God, retaining the place in life the Lord has assigned, difficult, though it may be.

_____

_____

_____

What things might you need to sell, or what affections do you need to let go of, in order to "buy gold" from Christ?

Self

_____

_____

Purified Hearts

DAY TWO

Day 2+3

EZEKIEL—HARD HEARTS

Ezekiel was a prophet during the time Israel was in exile in Babylonia. He was the son of a priest, and was taken into captivity in 597 B.C. After five years of exile, he was situated near a river in Babylonia when the heavens opened and he began seeing visions of God. Many of his visions were bizarre and mysterious to say the very least. Some of the details are quite difficult to interpret even to this day, but the underlying message comes through loud and clear. His message was to a rebellious people who were being disciplined by God because of their hardened hearts. Ezekiel prophesied for over twenty-two years speaking strong words of both judgment and restoration to God's people. Today we will study several passages from Ezekiel to see what God would say to us about our hearts.

📖 Read Ezekiel 2:1–7 and 3:7–11. What do you think is a primary symptom of a hard heart? How can we tell if our hearts are hard? How do we listen to His voice?

A) not listening (what does that mean?) B) if we are willing or not to listen c)

_____

Did You Know?

OUT OF TOUCH WITH REALITY

The phrase *"and you shall know that I am the Lord"* is repeated forty-seven times in Ezekiel. A person with a hard heart refuses to acknowledge Christ is Lord.

A person with a hard heart or a rebellious spirit refuses to listen to God. Such a person has grown calloused to spiritual things and closes himself or herself off from God's word. Verse 10 says we are to take His words into our hearts and listen closely. Verse 2 describes how the Spirit entered into Ezekiel's heart and caused him to stand at attention, ready to listen. We should pray that the Spirit would do the same for us.

📖 Read Ezekiel 11:12. What does acknowledging His lordship mean to you, and with what is it contrasted in this verse?

to obey His commands vs to give in to the world (Nations) around me — then it was (like Taiwan) other gods.

Like the Israelites in Ezekiel's day, there are many in the church today who need to know that Christ is Lord. We know Him as our Savior, but we are still conformed to the world around us rather than acknowledging His rule and reign in every area of our lives. We pick and choose the parts of Christianity that are easy, but our hearts are still hard when it comes to complete surrender to the will of God.

📖 Read Ezekiel 14:3–8. Why do you think a person with a hard heart turns to idols? What are some idols before us today, and why do we turn to them?

A) selfishness B) anything that replaces God, food, money, self, sex, work, sports, spouses, they only want to hear what they think it should be.

We are created to love and to worship. We must love something. If we harden our hearts toward God, we will always turn to something else. Don't be deceived. Just because we are Christians does not mean we are immune to temptation by idols. Every moment of every day we are bombarded by choices that pit our faith and desire to listen to God against the idols of this world. Most of the time, we don't even recognize the battle. Without a second thought our rebellious attitudes steer us toward the pleasures we think will meet our needs or bring us comfort or relief. From there it doesn't take long for a habit to become an addiction, and an addiction to become bondage.

marilyn

Another reason we turn to idols is the satisfaction they bring is usually immediate and we do not want to wait on the Lord. It is like the difference between fast food and the feast on the table of a faithful farmer. Idols promise a quick fix, but God's feast comes at the end of a long process of interaction with God and His people. A pure heart is willing to work and wait for the better meal.

📖 Read Ezekiel 11:18–20 and 18:30–32. How do we get a new heart? Clearly, it is a gift and not a result of works (see also Ephesians 2:8–9), yet what is our part according to these verses?

Repent and God will give you/me a new heart he will take the harden heart away

We would all be elated if the gift of a new or pure heart had no strings attached—if God would just zap us to perfection. It is true that our works and self-righteousness do nothing to purify our hearts, we must submit to the radical surgery of a heart transplant. Yet there is one work (if you would call it that) that God requires of us, and that is the work of repentance. We must turn away from our transgressions, cast away our idols, and set our hearts to love and obey God. Repentance is more than confession or simply admitting we are sinners. It is actually moving in a different direction. God does the work of changing us, but we must turn our faces toward Him.

📖 Read Ezekiel 33:30–32. Is it enough to hear the Word of the Lord? What kind of "gain" do you think these hearts are looking for? Try to put verse 32 into your own words, describing people of our day.

 *Put Yourself in Their Shoes*
ADDICTIONS

Many women have acknowledged their addictions to the following idols. Think about your own temptations in these areas and consider how much of a hold they have on you. How might it help you to make a conscious realization that the choice is between the idol and your desire for God?

- eating
- drinking or drugs
- entertainment (television, computer games, exercise, music, sports, etc.)
- sex or romance
- materialism/shopping

A) AND VS 31+32 put the words into practice. B) gain for self to get something for nothing.

What we have read from Ezekiel makes it clear that we must be attentive to spiritual matters before our hearts can be made pure. But these verses point out that just coming to hear a prophet speak (or coming to church or Bible study) proves that our hearts are pure—they can still be greedy. Our motivation is critical. If we come to church to be blessed, or to gain some new insight, or to get our prayers answered, or to be entertained, or to hang out with our friends, or to please the one who invited us—our hearts will not be changed. But if we come with repentance, with a deep desire to be changed, and a willingness to obey whatever the Lord tells us to do—God will purify our hearts.

📖 Read Ezekiel 36:22–23, 32 and 25–27. Why does God change hearts?

① For His glory — the sake of His Holy Name, holiness of His great Name, to show Himself Holy. ② Cleanse us of impurities

We easily fall into the error of thinking purification is all about us.

We easily fall into the error of thinking purification is all about us. We imagine God purifies our hearts so our lives will be better and our relationships healed. God's goals are much bigger, for He is out to save nations. A purified heart is a testimony to His grace and power. It is a vessel He can use for His kingdom. He wants to vindicate the holiness of His great name. A heart cleansed of its filthiness is free to obey its Master. When a heart of stone is removed and replaced with a heart of flesh, God's Spirit finds a new dwelling place, and the kingdom is carried to new horizons.

APPLY Judging from your openness to listening to the Lord, would you see your heart as hard or pure? Do you think it can be both to some degree?

① somewhere inbetween. ② somethings can be hardened heart while others are a pure heart with degrees in both areas

Are there areas in your life where you still do not recognize that Christ is Lord? How is God dealing with those hard places in your heart?

What idols are you tempted to turn to? When are you most susceptible to your idols?

① feel good things to make me feel good. ② when my wounds are exposed

What motivates you to attend church?

the presense of other believers worshiping like I do.

why do I attend the church I do?

What motivates you to desire a pure heart?

to be more Christ like to love like Jesus Christ does.

HOSEA—ADULTEROUS HEARTS

Some of us don't struggle with a hard heart, but rather one that loves too much. We can get into as much trouble as our hard-hearted sisters at the other end of the spectrum. We think our hearts are big enough to love more than the limits God puts on us. We think we can love our spouses and our lovers. We think we can love God and the world. We think we can hold on to numerous addictions all at the same time. That way we can turn in any direction and always find relief. But God is a jealous God and will not tolerate adulterous hearts.

Hosea was a prophet who knew the depths of love, the pain of betrayal, and the power of forgiveness. He was taught about the heart or longings of God by experiencing a marriage to an adulterous wife. Then he was led to preach to the people of God in an effort to turn their hearts back to the Lord.

Read Hosea 1:2–11. What conflicted feelings are found in those betrayed by unfaithfulness? Why do you think God wanted Hosea to experience them all? How do the names of Hosea's children reflect God's anger and pain?

① love/hate,
② to understand how God felt

③ sad

This first chapter of Hosea is a synopsis of the book, introducing the characters, the pain, the tragedy, and yet the possibility of hope for a people who have adulterous hearts. The main characters are God and His people illustrated in the marriage of Hosea and Gomer. God seems to want Hosea to understand His personal pain and anguish over the rejection of those He loves so he can preach with passion to a people on the brink of severe discipline. Did you notice both the wrath and compassion of God? Anyone who has experienced unfaithfulness in marriage knows what it is like to want both revenge and reconciliation, to remember both tender moments and fierce anger, to love and hate—all mixed together in a boiling cauldron of pain.

📖 Read Hosea 4:1, 6, 10–11; and 5:4. What was the root problem among God's people in Hosea's day? Do you see a similar problem today? How can we avoid a similar consequence (see Hosea 6:3 and 10:12)?

①prostitution ②yes U.S.A.
③acknowledge the Lord
Repent.

The Israelites no longer knew the Lord, and they had become enslaved to their addictions. How many of us truly know the Lord and are hungry for Him above all else? Can you say with Paul (Philippians 3:8) that you consider everything else rubbish compared to knowing Christ? John Piper suggests that the lost discipline of fasting could help us regain a better balance in our lives. Think and pray about the following quotes from his excellent book, *Hunger for God.*

> Fasting is guarding my heart from alien affections. . . . [It] is a test to see what desires control us. . . . Fasting keeps the preferring faculty on alert. Many small acts of preferring fellowship with God above food can form a habit of communion and contentment. . . . Fasting reveals the measure of food's mastery over us—or television or computers or whatever we submit to again and again to conceal the weakness of our hunger for God. . . . [We fast] not because we are hungry for something we have not experienced, but because the new wine of Christ's presence is so real and so satisfying that we want more—a hunger for all the fullness of God aroused by the aroma of Jesus' love. . . . so satisfied in Him that the power of all other allurements is broken.[5]

I believe there are so many distractions in our culture today, that there is no way we can truly press on to know the Lord without fasting. Fasting helps make us serious about our desire to know Him more. It is part of breaking up the fallow ground. The only way to "sow righteousness" is to spend intimate time with the Lord. We know our own attempts at righteousness will get us nowhere. His Spirit rains the fruit of righteousness upon us.

📖 Read Hosea 2:6–7, 14–17, and 19–20. To what lengths is God willing to go in order to recapture our wayward hearts? How does thinking about God's perseverance help us interpret some of the troubles we experience in life? How does Deuteronomy 30:6 describe what is happening?

① Block paths, wall us in, lead us to the desert and then talk to us sweetly.
② gives me hope for my kids.
③ cutting off extra we don't need to ~~draw~~ love him with all our hearts, soul and life. (more abundantly)

Extra Mile
HOSEA 11:1-9

Read Hosea 11:1–9 to get a picture of how God sees His relationship with the people of Israel, and how He yearns over them and feels such anguish because of their adulteries.

Fasting isn't always living alone with God. At times fasting alone can't beat time.

He loves Thee too little who loves anything together with Thee which he loves not for Thy sake.

—St Augustine
The Confessions

Deuteronomy 30:6 speaks of God *"circumcising our hearts."* This refers to God cutting away all the idols, the addictions, the loves of our lives that pull us away from Him. When He doesn't answer our prayers or give us what we want, He might be hedging us in—protecting us from loves that can ultimately hurt us. When he leads us to the Valley of Achor—or troubles, He always provides a door of hope. He wants us to see Him as our husband rather than be mastered by all our idols. When we allow suffering to do its work of refining our hearts, we are able to love Him more fully and know Him more intimately.

📖 Read Hosea 14:1–9. Describe both the repentance Hosea suggests and God's response outlined in these verses. Write out your own words of repentance for your spiritual adultery. See also James 4:4–10.

[handwritten: Forgive all our sins and receive us graciously. Assyria cannot save us. We will not mount war-horses. We will never again say "Our gods" to what our own hands have made.]

[handwritten margin: more from God than from repentance]

The only words we can take with us when we enter the presence of God are words of repentance. We have stumbled because of our iniquity, and we need His grace to cleanse us and receive us. We need to forsake our pride and come for mercy alone. James reminds us that we are all adulterers, that friendship with the world is such a big part of our lives. We commit spiritual adultery every time we choose anything the world offers over knowing Him more intimately. As verses 5 and 6 in the New King James Version make clear, the Spirit yearns jealously for our hearts, but we proudly withhold them and go our own ways. We let the devil trap us in our addictions, and we fail to draw near to God. Our divided hearts need to be purified.

APPLY What tempts you most to stray from an undivided love and devotion to Christ? *[handwritten: Where am I not devoted to Christ?]*

FRIEND OF THE WORLD?

Adulterers and adulteresses! Do you not know that friendship with the world is enmity with God? Whoever therefore wants to be a friend of the world makes himself an enemy of God. Or do you think that the Scripture says in vain, "The Spirit who dwells in us yearns jealously"? (James 4:4–5 NKJV)

Have you ever pitted your love for God up against a lesser love? Did that help you to choose your love for God rather than the idol? How effective might that prove to be the next time you are tempted by spiritual adultery?

What loves tend to divide your heart?

MARY MAGDALENE—MISJUDGED HEARTS

I n the movie *The Magdalene,* the story is told of four Irish girls who are sent to a convent for girls who have had babies out of wedlock. Each of the girls was stigmatized as an evil, unredeemable woman and was given no grace nor hope for a future. The name of the convent was "Sisters of Magdala." At one point in the movie this name is explained by describing Mary Magdalene as a wicked woman who gave herself sexually to any man she met. Today we are going to look at what the Bible actually teaches about Mary Magdalene and decide for ourselves if she was, on the contrary, a most amazing example of a woman with a pure heart.

📖 Read Luke 8:1–3. How do these verses introduce us to Mary? How was her heart made pure? What two things did she do after that?

_____

_____

_____

_____

Mary was from the city of Magdala, and had evidently been plagued for years by seven demons. These verses tell us Jesus healed her and that she joined the twelve apostles in following Him as he traveled to the cities and villages in Palestine. She also may have been one of the women who contributed to His financial support.

📖 Read John 19:25. What do the three Mary's have in common? Why do you think they stood together at the foot of the cross?

_____

_____

_____

_____

Contrary to Dan Brown's contention in his novel, *The DaVinci Code,* there is absolutely no evidence that Mary was anything but a recipient of Christ's miraculous power to free her from demon possession, and to bring her salvation by His death on the cross. Like the other Marys who watched the crucifixion, I think she depended on the support of her friends to endure the horror of what she saw. Mary Magdalene obviously loved Jesus, but only as her master and teacher in earlier times, and later she would love Him as her Savior. Any suggestion that she had a physical relationship with Him is absurd. I wonder if our culture's obsession with sex doesn't make it difficult for some to imagine love without it. To think Jesus was married to Mary reveals a hardness of heart that will not accept the kind of love that Jesus offers.

📖 Read Mark 15:40, 41, and 47. What do these verses tell us about Mary?

_____

_____

_____

Besides identifying Mary among the women who watched the crucifixion, Mark tells us she was one who followed and ministered or waited on Jesus during His life and travels. Her desire to be with Jesus and not let Him out of her sight put her into some dangerous situations. She must have been a determined risk taker to spy on Joseph of Arimathea as he buried Christ's body—while the rest of the disciples were cowering in fear. Nothing could quench the love Mary felt for Jesus. She was so focused on her Lord that she risked everything for Him.

📖 Read Mark 16:1–11. Why do you think Mary was the first one to "see God" in His resurrected body? Do you suppose it might have something to do with the purity of her heart?

_____

_____

_____

Our beatitude for this week promises that the pure in heart will see God. Remember part of the definition we gave at the beginning of this chapter, "purity of heart is single-eyed devotion." Maybe because Mary's heart had been cleansed of seven evil spirits, she was left with a childlike attitude and faith that allowed her to love Jesus without distraction. She was so devoted to Him, there was no room in her heart for other things.

Mark's account of the first few hours after the resurrection indicates that everyone but Mary had doubt or fear in their hearts. According to verse eight, the other women fled. John tells us Mary stayed behind, totally determined to find Christ. Mark tells us that even when she told the weeping disciples that she had seen Christ, they refused to believe it. Obviously, their feelings of despair would not let them accept the truth.

📖 Read John 20:6–18. What can we learn from John's account about Mary? What do you think of her tenacity and pursuit of Christ? In contrast, how do lesser things distract us?

_____

_____

_____

_____

Peter and John saw the empty tomb and, according to verse eight, "believed" that something happened to Christ's body but verse nine tells us they did not yet understand the resurrection and so they went home. I admit, often I just "go home" instead of lingering in God's presence, or waiting a bit longer for Him to reveal Himself to me. I cut short my prayer time when I begin to think about all the other things that need to be done. Or I walk past a hurting woman who needs my love, because I am not focused on the love of Christ, but on my need to get home.

But Mary stayed. She was willing to endure the pain of weeping longer and seeking further. Her heart was pure—filled with a love that would not let go. When Jesus tells her to stop clinging to Him, He is not putting down her tenacity but is simply explaining that His physical presence would soon be no longer hers to enjoy, for He was going to ascend to His Father.

Jesus' tender love and mercy towards Mary is totally missed in the film *The Magdalene.* In that movie God is depicted as a punishing tyrant who is bringing shame and humiliation on women caught in sin. Rather than being a place of grace and forgiveness, the church is portrayed as a place of judgment and torture. Imagine Christ's voice speaking your name as He spoke Mary's. He sees your heart—cleansed by His own blood shed for you. There is no condemnation or judgment. There is only love and grace. Although we may long for a physical embrace, as did Mary, we need to understand and accept that until we have also received our resurrected bodies, the embrace of His love needs to stay in the spiritual realm. But that does not in any way reduce the reality of His love.

📖 Read 1 John 3:18–21. How often do we misjudge our own hearts? Do we ever condemn ourselves like the church in the movie condemned Mary Magdalene?

_____

_____

_____

_____

_____

_____

"Reassure our hearts before Him. . . . if our hearts do not condemn us, we have boldness before God."

1 John 3:19, 21 (NIV)

When we love in deed and truth, our hearts are reassured that we belong to Him and can rest in His presence. But when our "hearts condemn us" through our lack of love, we would have reason to despair and even wonder if we are saved. Thankfully, God is greater than our hearts, so when we lack the love we need, we can come to Him and ask Him to fill us with His love.

I wonder if some churches focus too much on the evil in our hearts rather than seeing our hearts as redeemed and in the process of renewal. Do we hold on to the identity of sinners so much that we lose sight of the possibility of having hearts filled with love—pure hearts?

Nelson Mandela is quoted as saying:

> Our deepest fear is not that we are inadequate. Our deepest fear is that we are powerful beyond measure. It is our light, not our darkness, that most frightens us. We ask ourselves, "Who am I to be brilliant, gorgeous, talented and fabulous [or pure in heart]? Actually, who are you not to be? You are a child of God. Your playing small doesn't serve the world. There's nothing enlightened about shrinking so that other people won't feel insecure around you. We were born to manifest the glory of God that is within us.[6] (text in brackets mine)

Having a pure heart does not mean we are without sin. This beatitude is not requiring us to be sinless; it is encouraging us to love Jesus with abandon. It is holding up the possibility of, and even promise for, hearts that have been purified by Christ and are therefore filled with love for Him and for others around them. Those possessing a heart like this will never condemn themselves, and they will have confidence before God no matter what others, in their misjudgment, may say of them. When we stand with boldness, right next to Mary Magdalene, then we, too, will see God.

APPLY How has Satan twisted the truth of Mary's (and our) need and Christ's love?

_____

_____

_____

Is your church a place of judgment or grace?

_____

_____

How has your understanding of "pure in heart" changed? Can you see your heart being purified?

_____

_____

_____

Do you think you fear your own light, purity, and power? How does that fear manifest itself?

_____

_____

_____

_____

THE HEART OF JESUS

Purified Hearts

DAY FIVE

The heart of Jesus is pure. It is filled with pure love. It is totally focused on doing the will of His Father. It is not divided, distracted, or devoted to anything or anyone other than God. He is the only one born without a desperately wicked heart. He is the only one whose heart has never been pulled into idolatry or the love of lesser gods. His love never grows cold. It never fails. Somehow in the mystery of our unity with Him, the heart of Jesus is implanted into us, and we are enabled by the power of His Spirit to love as He loves. As you study the heart of Jesus, be encouraged that He puts His heart in you and gives you the choice to live out of that heart.

📖 Read 2 Corinthians 5:21; Hebrews 4:15–16; 7:25–26; and 1 Peter 1:18–19. Why is it important for us that Jesus has a pure heart?

_____

_____

_____

_____

Think about it, if Jesus' heart was not pure, we could not become the righteousness of God in Him. Only a High Priest with a pure heart could bring us into the throne room of God. If His heart were not pure, He would not

Doctrine
ATONEMENT

Atonement is the process of bringing those who are estranged into unity. Christ's work of atonement was His dealing with the problem posed by the sin of man, to bring and keep sinners in right relation with God. He did this by His perfect life of obedience, His sacrificial death on the cross—paying the ransom, taking our place, redeeming us from the curse of the law, and by His resurrection which empowers us to become true sons and daughters who can continue to live in right relationship with God.

be able to save us or intercede for us. Just as all the sacrifices in the Old Testament had to be without blemish, the perfect Lamb of God that they represented had to be pure in heart. Our atonement is based on Christ's perfect sacrifice.

📖 Read Matthew 12:34–35. How would you define the heart according to Jesus' description?

_____

_____

_____

_____

Jesus' words help us to see how our hearts have a direct effect on what we do and say. Our affections and desires are the real determinates of our words and actions. What we love is what motivates us. Our deepest affections and desires are harbored much the same way items are stored in a treasure chest—only our hearts can hold both good and bad treasures or affections. Jesus makes a corollary statement in Matthew 6:21, *"for where your treasure is there will your heart be also."*

📖 Read Ephesians 5:25–27. What is the treasure of Jesus' heart? How does He show His love?

_____

_____

_____

_____

I think these verses show us that the treasure of Jesus' heart is the purified church. He loves us, gave Himself for us, sanctifies us, cleanses us, wants us to be holy and blameless, and longs for the day He can present us to Himself in all our glory. What if Jesus' treasure became our treasure as well? How would that change what we say and do? I think there would be a movement away from preoccupation with how we look, what we own, how our homes are decorated, what our children are doing, and more investment in discipleship and heart change (in our own lives, our children's lives, and in our churches.)

📖 Read Ephesians 3:14–19. Why do we need to be *"strengthened with power . . . in the inner man"*? What comprehension needs such strength and why?

_____

_____

_____

_____

Before we can treasure what Christ treasures, before we can love others as He loves them, before we can even comprehend the love of Christ, our hearts (or inner person) must be strengthened with power from the Holy Spirit. I know my own heart is so in need of His power and grace—I haven't even begun to plumb the depths of His love for me. I need to pray this prayer in Ephesians for myself every day. But I pray it for others as well: the woman who stays away from church or Bible study because she doesn't feel worthy; the girl who struggles with addictions and can't let them go; the friend who is trapped in an unhealthy relationship because she can't face loneliness; the one who is depressed and hopeless—they all need to be strengthened in the inner man . . . to know the love of Christ which surpasses knowledge. If we really knew how much He loves us, and what He wants for us, and longs to do for us, so much of our stress and worry would just fall away.

📖 Read Matthew 13:10–17. What did Jesus teach in this passage about seeing God? What do you think Jesus is describing when He mentions hearts becoming dull? Why is it necessary to understand with our hearts (see verse 15)? In Ephesians 1:17 and 18 Paul prays that we would be given a spirit of wisdom and revelation so that the eyes of our hearts would be enlightened. Do you think this is a similar thing to what Jesus is talking about?

_____

_____

_____

_____

If we would know the mysteries of the kingdom, we must pray that our hearts be renewed. If our dulled hearts or spiritual senses keep us from seeing, understanding, and repenting, we should plead for God to change them. By nature, there is such a disconnect between my mind and heart that I can deal with all the data, arrange the facts in logical order, report the truth in a passionless way, and put it all neatly away without my heart ever engaging in any of it. On my own I am dull and insensitive. I need a supernatural way of seeing to take me into love.

📖 Read John 17:6–8 and 20–26. How do we see God? What do you think it means to be one with the Father and the Son? If we are in Them, and They are in us (verses 21 and 23), how might this purify our hearts? What do you think it means to be perfected in unity? What does love have to do with our hearts? What happens to our hearts when they are filled with the same love that the Father has for the Son?

_____

_____

_____

_____

This side of heaven, we cannot actually see God, we can only know His name. And that, according to verse 26, has been made known to us by Jesus. The Spirit, in the body of Christ, accomplishes the purifying of our hearts through relationship and intimacy with the Father, through the Son. Loving God and loving the brethren with the love He puts in our hearts purifies our hearts. The more we love, the more love we are given, the more changed we become.

I think being perfected in unity is a transformational thing that happens when we allow the love of the Trinity to define our relationship with one another. Do you realize what Jesus is praying here? Verse 21 implies we can be one in the same way that the Father and the Son are in each other's lives! Can you wrap your heart and mind around that? In case you didn't get it the first time He repeats it in verse 22. We can be one, just as They are one.

It all happens when the love that the Father had for the Son is put in us. Go back and read verses 21 and 22 again and again until the idea of being one seeps deep into your heart. Jesus is praying for something absolutely amazing here. Is it your prayer as well?

We can be one just as the Father, Son, and Holy Spirit are one.

 What are some ways you can open yourself more to the love of Christ?

_____

_____

_____

What happens when our love for lesser gods fills our hearts?

_____

_____

Why do you think the Bible emphasizes the condition of our hearts so much?

_____

_____

_____

Have you "seen God"? In what way? Describe your experience.

_____

_____

_____

Spend some time in prayer.

I praise you my Father for the purity of Your Son, Jesus Christ. I thank You for allowing me to see Him with the eyes of my heart. He is so precious in His uniqueness, so beautiful in His radiance, and so full of truth and kindness. Please continue to give me a vision of His glory.

Lord, I confess my heart is still filled with folds. So much is hidden from others and even myself. I know it is plagued with hypocrisy. Its motives are mixed and sometimes evil. My heart is so far from single-eyed devotion to Christ and it needs Your cleansing and careful circumcision. Please forgive me and continue to purify my heart.

Please help me to live out of my redeemed heart. Please strengthen my inner person to know Christ's love in a way that frees me to love others. Free my heart from the fears that keep me small and weak. Lord, I long to manifest Your glory and reveal Christ's love to others.

I know that Satan is constantly accusing me and trying to fill my heart with false guilt. Deliver me from his evil lies and help me to stand firm against him. Reassure my heart before You that You are not condemning me. Give me the boldness to stand before You dressed in the righteousness of Christ.

I pray that I can go from this place with a pure heart that can love in truth and action. I pray this for Your glory. May all I do glorify You. Thine is the Kingdom, power and glory forever. Amen.

Works Cited

1. W. E. Vine, *Expository Dictionary of New Testament Words* (Old Tappan, NJ: Fleming H. Revell Company, 1966), 3:231.

2. Ibid, 2:207.

3. Martin Lloyd-Jones, *Studies in the Sermon on the Mount* (Grand Rapids, MI: Wm. B. Eerdmans Publishing Co., 2000), 111.

4. Sharon A. Hersh, *Brave Hearts* (Colorado Springs, CO: WaterBrook Press, 2001), 6, 10, 16, 22, 171.

5. John Piper, *Hunger for God* (Wheaton, IL: Crossway Books, 1997), 62, 58, 19, 20, 42.

6. John Eldredge, *Waking the Dead* (Nashville, TN: Thomas Nelson, Inc., 2003), 87.

7. L. L. Morris in *The New Bible Dictionary* (Wm. B. Eerdmans Publishing Co., 1973), 107–109. Definition of "atonement" on p. 102 a combination of ideas from Morris and my brother-in-law, Dr. David Morton.

Notes

Peaceful Hearts

*"Blessed are the peacemakers,
for they shall be called the sons of God" (Matthew 5:9)*

Our time with Samantha was short, but intense. When she first came to our church she explained she was seeking to renew her relationship with God, but that was bringing conflict to many of her relationships in the gay community where she had been an active spokesperson for many years. While ministering to AIDS patients, she contracted the disease as a result of an accidental needle prick. Facing death, her greatest fear was that she would die alone. Peace seemed far away and unattainable as she felt cut off from everyone.

"I could never forgive my mother. Don't even go there. You don't know what she did to me!" Samantha was adamant and refused to listen to my pleas to consider the blessing that could come from peacemaking. Indeed, it was a sad and sordid tale that explained how she got where she was. But I knew her healing would not come without forgiveness, and I watched as God chipped away at her anger and resentment over the next few weeks. A few days later she visited a small group meeting, and of course, the topic for the evening was forgiveness. The suggestion was made to make a list of grievances, and at the next meeting they had some kind of ceremony of burying their lists under a special rock. She told me she had decided to focus on her bitterness towards her mother.

Samantha and I didn't talk again about the peacemaking process with her mother. So recently, I called her mother to find out what had happened in the few weeks they had together before Samantha passed away. She explained that their reunion came after a long, six-year period of absolutely no communication

Samantha...

...making peace

whatsoever, and that their relationship had been severely strained long before that. But one day out of the blue Sam called and asked if she and a friend from church could come up to her mountain cabin for a brief visit. They didn't stay long, and Samantha spent most of the time outside stockpiling wood. Her mother said, "We were getting reacquainted after so many years, and while fragile it was very good. She came two more weekends, and I have written an account of our time together and would be glad to share it with you." The paragraphs below are adapted from her journal.

During the course of those weekends, Sam asked me several times: "How are we doing?" I told her that as far as I was concerned, great. On one occasion, she asked: "So, how are we doing?"

"What do you mean?" I replied.

"Us. How are 'We' doing?"

"I. . . I. . . I'm overwhelmed. You are being so good to me; you have been so angry with me for so long. What has made the difference?"

"God."

"Can you say more about that?"

"I just decided that I could either be angry the rest of my life, or I could let God have my anger, and I could be whole."

One day, when I was sitting at the kitchen table and Sam was over at the stove, preparing dinner, our backs to one another. I sighed, not realizing it. She said, "What?" I said, "What, what?" She said, "You sighed; what was that about?" I finally told her that I had just been wishing we had had this kind of a relationship for much longer; that we had lived without one another for nearly twenty-five years." She said: "Come here," standing over me with her arms out wide. I let myself cry while we hugged one another tightly, all the while, Sam saying, "It's okay, Mom; it's okay."

On her last Saturday with me, Sam felt it was important to leave a few hours earlier than planned; it appeared there was a trace of an infection on her arm. As she was leaving, I said: "I'll walk down to the car with you." She said, "No, Mom, let's say good-bye here; I know how hard it is for you to manage the stairs." As we stood at the top of the stairs saying good-bye, I thanked her for all she had done for me, but mostly for bringing herself to me; it being really special. "There's something so special about a daughter that is beyond words; there is a place that only a daughter can fill. You have always been my joy, Samantha." She beamed, turned, and headed to her car. As she pulled out of the drive, she rolled down her window, calling out above the sound of the river, "I just may live to be 80!" A little while later, glancing out the window, I saw her stopped in front of my next-door neighbor's house, with him (the "Pastor Dude" in town) leaning at the car window. They must have talked for ten minutes. I'm thinking: "She was in such a hurry to get out of here; I wonder what that is all about." Weeks later, John told me that she was telling him how sick she was, and that she was asking him to check on me every once in awhile, in the future, to make sure I had enough cordwood and other essentials. He told me that she was so overjoyed at healing things with me, that she could hardly believe it.

During the final six months she had with us, Samantha experienced the love and peace of the family of God, making peace with God, her mother and father, and with many Christians who extended grace and love to her. Hospital personnel were amazed and sometimes frustrated by the number of people who wanted to be with her as she lay dying. Her funeral was an amaz-

Word Study
PEACEMAKER

"[A peacemaker is] one who resolves conflict by facing up to her own faults, by showing a [sister her] fault, by being committed to restoring damaged relationships, all for the glory of God. Instead of reacting to disputes in a confused, defensive, or angry manner, a peacemaker learns to manage conflict confidently and constructively."[1]

ing testimony to the love and peace she found in her final days. Even her friends from the gay community commented that her final six months were the best of her life. She is now at perfect peace among the sons and daughters of God in heaven.

A peacemaker is willing to follow the wisdom of God in bringing peace on earth. God is in the business of reconciliation, and He wants His children to share in His business.

JACOB—MAKING PEACE WITHIN

Jacob, that Old Testament patriarch, was a duplicitous troublemaker. He connived against his brother for the birthright, then later, with his mother's help, he deceived his dying father in an effort to receive the blessing. Like a pitiful coward, Jacob fled the scene of his crime rather than work for reconciliation with Esau. Jacob was a schemer, but God continued to work positive change in Jacob's heart, and over time Jacob evolved into a peacemaker. As you study some scenes from Jacob's life after he left home, watch closely for how God dealt with him, and how he ultimately brought him to peace.

📖 Read Genesis 28:10–22. How did Jacob respond to the love and promises God gave him at Bethel? How does the promise of God's presence bring peace?

A) He made a (vow) commitment to God. He made a pillar (like tabernacle)

B) _____

_____

At this point in the story Jacob has fled for his life. He fears his brother's retribution and is beginning to reap the consequences of years of conflict and deceit. Circumstances have reduced Jacob to complete poverty and he is now open to God's love and covenant promises. All true peace begins with making peace with God. Jacob's worship at Bethel is his first step towards becoming a peacemaker.

📖 Read Genesis 29. How does Jacob respond to others in this passage? Would you say he is a peacemaker yet?

So So

So So

Here Jacob is slowly learning the important peacemaking concept of compromise. But he hasn't arrived just yet. He is willing to work with Laban and come up with a win-win solution to their differing priorities. While Jacob is hardly a mature peacemaker in his dealings with Laban, at least He doesn't cut and run like he did with Esau. Instead Jacob is willing to respect Laban, a deceiver in his own right. Jacob's relationship with Leah, however, reveals that he still may be struggling with self-centered tendencies that prevent him from loving with God's love.

📖 Read Genesis 31:1–13, 20, 36, and 41–42. How does Jacob respond to his father-in-law's unfair dealings with him? How does that compare with 1 Peter 2:21–23?

Jacob allowed him to treated unfair

Same

Put Yourself in Their Shoes
LEAH

Imagine what it must have been like for Leah. How would you have responded to being forced to marry your sister's lover, and having to share him with her? Which of the following would you be?

- A bitter, resentful woman
- A jealous and angry wife
- One who denies the reality of a grievous situation
- A peacemaker

In his dealings with Laban, Jacob comes pretty close to following Christ's example for responding to those who deal unfairly with us. Genesis 31:6–7 show us that Jacob was like Christ in that he did not *"revile in return"* for being reviled (1 Peter 2:23). And like Christ, Jacob *"uttered no threats"* (1 Peter 2:23). Jacob also trusted God to judge between Laban and himself (see Genesis 31:41–42) and didn't try to manage and manipulate as he had before. But Genesis 31:20 shows us the one place he failed.

Unlike Christ, we cannot say of Jacob in his departure from Laban that no *"deceit was found in his mouth"* (1 Peter 2:22). Through Jacob's troubles with Laban, he gradually learns how to be a peacemaker, but the hardest lesson for him to learn, and probably the hardest one for most of us, is to always speak the truth in love. Jacob's name means "deceiver," and this name was quite fitting, because deception was his besetting sin.

📖 Read Genesis 31:43–55. What can we learn from this peacemaking ritual?

I see four very important peacemaking lessons illustrated in this passage. The first is Jacob's willingness to listen to Laban without contradicting or correcting him. Laban's statement in verse 43 was not true, but when Jacob allowed him to say it, it probably helped to diffuse anger. Actually, if you look carefully, you will notice Laban does most of the talking throughout the peacemaking process. Humbly letting someone else fully express herself without being defensive is important. The second factor that should be noted and imitated is the practice of making a "heap of witness." Finding a way to help both parties remember the agreements made in the peacemaking process is very important. Most of us are not into stacking stones and pillars, but we should at least try to think of appropriate ways to record and remember the peace that is made. Verse 47 points out a third key factor in peacemaking. Like this one, many of our disagreements arise from semantics. If we can't agree on the definition of terms or on what to call something, we sometimes need to agree to disagree. Notice Jacob does it again in verse 53, when Laban suggests they swear by the God of Abraham and the God of Nahor, Jacob doesn't make a big point of disagreement, but simply swears by *"the fear of his father Isaac,"* which was the name he used for the true God. He doesn't let Laban put words in his mouth, but he doesn't make an issue of it either. The fourth key factor in peacemaking that I see in this story is that Jacob puts together a meal to celebrate their unity and seal their reconciliation. Eating together has always been a symbol of peace and unity.

communion

📖 Read Genesis 32:9–12. What can we learn from Jacob's prayer for peace?

give God the credit – show humility, ask for help, express true feelings, quote God.

God must have used the peacemaking process with Laban to teach Jacob to trust Him more. He now knows to pray first. He now knows to pray first. However it happened, Jacob now knows to pray first. John Newton, the author of the famous hymn "Amazing Grace," wrote the following about the importance of prayer in the peacemaking process:

> As to your opponent, I wish, that, before you set pen to paper against him, and during the whole time you are preparing your answer, you may commend him by earnest prayer to the Lord's teaching and blessing. This practice will have a direct tendency to conciliate your heart to love and pity him; and such a disposition will have a good influence upon every page you write. . . . [If he is a believer,] in a little while you will meet him in heaven; he will then be dearer to you than the nearest friend you have upon earth is to you now. Anticipate that period in your thoughts. . . . [If he is an unconverted person,] he is a more proper object of your compassion than your anger. Alas! "He knows not what he does." But you know who has made you to differ [1 Corinthians 4:7].[2]

📖 Read Genesis 32:24–32. Why do you think it is sometimes necessary for us to wrestle with God? How does that lead to peace and blessing?

I understood the passages as Jacob being the winner of having self strength, it was only supernatural that overpowered Jacob.

God has to cripple me before I am humbled enough to let overpowered peace & blessing happen?

In answer to Jacob's prayer for peace, a mysterious assailant wrestles with him to deal with the last vestiges of his pride and self-sufficiency. Genesis 32:24 identifies the assailant as "a man" (NKJV capitalizes the first letter in man). Hosea 12:4 identifies the visitor as *the angel* (with the first letter of "angel" also capitalized in the NKJV). Most likely this mysterious figure is "the Angel of the LORD," a spiritual being many feel is a preincarnate appearance of Jesus Christ. Before changing him from a deceiver to the father of the nation of Israel, God needed to cripple Jacob's natural strength and cause him to depend more on supernatural strength. The fight represents a battle of surrender. We must all come to the place of surrender before we can be peacemakers.

📖 Read Genesis 33:1–11. What effect do you think Jacob's wrestling match the night before had on the favorable outcome of his meeting with his estranged brother, Esau? Why?

_____

_____

_____

_____

Jacob comes to Esau a humbled and broken man. (Verse 3 says he bowed to the ground seven times.) The last time he saw Esau, Jacob would have been saying something along the lines of, "I have acted shrewdly because I need what is yours." This time he essentially says, "God has dealt graciously with me, and I have enough." If we would see peace made in all our relationships, we must first and foremost approach those in our midst in humility, completely dependent on the grace of God.

APPLY Do you feel at peace within, or are there issues in your life God still needs to touch—like He touched Jacob's hip? How might you seek the Lord's help in addressing these areas?

_____

_____

_____

_____

Just as God used some of Jacob's difficult relationships to deal with his heart, how has He used various human relationships to show you what He wants to do in your heart?

_____

_____

_____

How would your rate your level of humility? (Warning: those who credit themselves with ample humility may in fact be struggling with pride.)

_____

_____

_____

Peaceful Hearts

DAY TWO

BARNABAS—MAKING PEACE WITH OTHERS

We are first introduced to Barnabas in Acts 4, but he is referred to as an apostle in Acts 14:14, which means that he followed Christ during His earthly ministry and was probably one of the seventy disciples who heard most of Christ's preaching. Barnabas must have been taking notes when Christ talked about being peacemakers, because he consistently followed His teaching on peace. There are two times when Jesus identifies who should be proactive in seeking peace. The first in Matthew 5:23–24 assigns the responsibility to one who has offended his brother. Then in Matthew 18:15 Christ delegates the responsibility of peacemaking to the one who has been sinned against. Notice as you read these accounts of the life of Barnabas that he was always quick to go and make peace, no matter who was at fault.

📖 Read Acts 4:34–37 and Philippians 2:3–8. What are some prerequisites for being a peacemaker?

_____

_____

_____

If we are to see Barnabas as a biblical example of a peacemaker, and it is clear he is presented as one, we can learn what it takes by these descriptions of him and of his Lord. Named "Joseph" at birth, he became known in the church as "Barnabas," a name that means "son of encouragement." His generous spirit and his care for the needy reveal why reveal why he was given this name. Barnabas brought encouragement to those who would otherwise be defeated by the difficulties of their circumstances. He exemplified the spirit of humility—the humility it takes to consider others more important than you. A peacemaker looks out for the interests of others as well as her own. Identifying the interests of all parties in any type of peacemaking effort is a key to resolving differences. Often, though the surface issues may look irreconcilable, if we go to the deeper interests of each party, unity can be found. For example, two women may have a conflict over which of two ministries is the best to pursue, but their deeper motivation is to serve the Lord. Rather than squabbling over which ministry is chosen, love and unity can be found in respecting each other's heart motivation, and then humbling themselves for obedience to the Lord.

📖 Read Acts 9:26–31. What was Barnabas' role in bringing peace to the church?

_____

_____

_____

Former persecutor of the church, Saul (before his name was changed to Paul) was trying to associate with the disciples, but these men did not initially accept him out of fear. Disunity is often the result of fear. Barnabas, however, embraced Saul, presented this new convert's miraculous story to the leadership of the early church, and ushered Saul into an active ministry in Jerusalem. I imagine Barnabas was part of the "brethren" who encouraged Saul to escape to Tarsus when persecution broke out. Barnabas was not only concerned for Saul's safety, but also for the peace of the church. He worked to bring unity and peace to all.

📖 Read Acts 11:19–26. How did Barnabas make peace in Antioch?

_____

_____

_____

Barnabas was sent from Jerusalem as an emissary of the leaders of the church to encourage new believers. His goodness, faith, and spiritual dependence on the Spirit were needed. The presence and encouragement of Barnabas brought peace to a new and growing church. His humility to recognize that Saul, not he, could best provide the teaching they needed brought just the right balance of truth and love for the believers in Antioch.

📖 Read Matthew 10:12–15 and Acts 13:49–52. There are times when peace can't be made; how did Barnabas ultimately respond in his conflict with the Jews of Pisidian Antioch?

_____

_____

_____

"The steadfast of mind Thou wilt keep in perfect peace, because he trusts in Thee."

Isaiah 26:3

This short account of Barnabas' relationship with unbelieving Jews illustrates that certain conflicts arise that cannot be resolved. We must let these situations go. "Shaking the dust off your feet" is a Jewish sign of displeasure and disassociation. Our call to love everyone does not necessarily mean we must associate with everyone. Peace is a two-way street, and we can only go as far as others will allow.

📖 Read Acts 15:1–12, 33. How did Paul and Barnabas make peace in this situation?

_____

_____

_____

In the midst of great dissension and debate, Paul and Barnabas stay committed to face-to-face communication. They are willing to make a trip all the way to Jerusalem to bring questions to the leadership. Then they stayed until peace had been established.

📖 Read Acts 15:36–41 and 13:13; Colossians 4:10; and 2 Timothy 4:11. What happened to break up the Paul/Barnabas team? Is division always bad? How was this rift resolved in later years? How does God multiply ministry by division?

_____

_____

_____

Paul and Barnabas couldn't agree on the involvement of Mark in their ministry, so they agreed to separate. Barnabas took Mark and traveled west. Paul hooked up with Silas and journeyed southeast. Satan may have thought he won a victory by causing disunity, but God used the split to multiply ministry. God's sovereignty in it all is reassuring—He can use even our petty disagreements to accomplish His will. But He also continues to work on our hearts to bring them around to peace, as He must have done with Paul and Mark. Paul's desire to have Mark by his side years later proves God does not let disunity last.

APPLY Is there anyone in your life that you know you have offended, but you have resisted talking to them about it? What can you do about it?

_____

_____

_____

_____

_____

_____

What are you prone to do when someone sins against you? Overlook it? Talk to others to see what they think? Fight? Flee? Pray?

_____

_____

_____

_____

What are some things you learned from Barnabas today that you want to implement in your own life?

_____

_____

_____

Paul—Making Peace in the Church

Paul probably learned many things from his mentor Barnabas. His long association with such an influential peacemaker taught Paul to value peace and unity. Today we will explore some of Paul's teaching on the unity of the church. Although he may not use the term "peacemaker," his emphasis on unity and peace imply the active work of peacemaking.

📖 Read Ephesians 2:11–22. Why is unity in the body of Christ so important? How is it accomplished according to this passage? What has Christ already done, and what must we do?

_____

_____

_____

Paul is contending for unity or the embrace of love that is based on the work of Christ. When we find ourselves at odds with one another we need to identify the enmity or hostility he refers to in verse 15. When we repent of the enmity and take it to the cross, Christ brings us near to our brothers and sisters. At the cross, Christ abolished the enmity, made a way for us to become one with our enemies, and established peace. We simply have to believe that Christ's work on the cross was the ultimate peacekeeping mission and live in the light of this fact as we deal with others. But as Miroslav Volf points out in his excellent book *Exclusion and Embrace,* it takes openness and self-giving to walk that path.

> From a Pauline perspective, the wall that divides is not so much "the difference" as it is enmity. . . . Neither the imposition of a single will nor the rule of a single law removes enmity. Hostility can be "put to death" only by self-giving. Peace is achieved "through the cross" and "by the blood." The cross is the foundation of Christian community. The crucified Messiah creates unity by giving His own self. . . . To find peace, people with self-enclosed identities need to open themselves for one another and give themselves to one another, yet without loss of the self or domination of the other.[4]

There is no excuse for allowing enmity to exist in the body of Christ, and yet I see it again and again in women who choose not to reconcile and still try to worship together. It makes no sense whatsoever, and it grieves the Holy Spirit. Jesus clearly taught his disciples in Matthew 5:24 that they should be reconciled with anyone who has something against them before they come to worship.

Word Study
ENMITY

Vine says "enmity" is the opposite of *agape*.[3] Webster says it is positive hatred which may be open or concealed . . . a desire to avoid or reject . . . a clash of temperaments leading to hostility . . . intense ill will and vindictiveness . . . bitter brooding over a wrong.

📖 Read Ephesians 4:1–6. What directions for unity does Paul give in this passage? (Be ready to share examples of ways you have experienced humility, gentleness, patience, forbearance, and diligence.) Why do you think Paul lists all the ways that we are one?

_____

_____

_____

_____

_____

Here, Paul teaches that we must find unity around the essentials and preserve unity around what is nonessential or debatable. The list of things that unite us includes the Trinity and the work of each person of the Trinity. The Holy Spirit makes us one body and gives us the grace we need to carry out our calling. Our Lord Christ gives us faith, and we are baptized into Him. God the Father is over all and through all and in all. We are united in and by the three persons of the Trinity. (Disunity is created whenever we make other things essential for fellowship or love among believers.) Think about things that your church or you might require for unity. Ask God to help you transfer the nonessential things to a list that will require humility, gentleness, patience, forbearance, and diligence. Give some thought as to why there is so much dissention in the church. Are the essentials we require for unity more than the essentials Paul gives to us in this passage?

📖 Read Colossians 3:8–15. What do we need to put aside in order to be peacemakers? What do we need to put on? How do you think that is accomplished?

_____

_____

_____

This passage is brimming with practical things we must do in order to be peacemakers. Putting aside our anger and gossip must come first. We probably haven't even begun to identify much of our conversation as gossip since we are so good at justifying our words and ourselves. We think we are free of lies, yet we don't stop to consider that much of our denial and pretense with one another is a form of lying. Again, we find our key word "renewal" in this passage, which underlines our need to be changed into Christ's likeness in order to become peacemakers. We must put on His righteousness by seeking to be one with Him. It is not merely a matter of trying to imitate Him. We must be united with Him and allow His compassion and gentleness to flow through us. Love is the perfect bond of unity. It is only His *agape* love in us that can accomplish our renewal and make us peacemakers.

📖 Read John 17:21 and Ephesians 4:16. What is the ultimate purpose of all peacemaking?

_____

_____

_____

Can you see the amazing implication of Christ's request? If He is asking that we become one even as the Trinity is one, it is an astonishing request. We talk about the great "Three-in-One"—is He saying our small group could be "ten in One," in similar fashion? Could our churches be "Two Hundred in One" or Two Thousand in One? That, of course, could not be possible without divine enablement and effective peacemaking! Paul understood what Christ refers to in John 17 and tells the Ephesians that the whole point of ministry is to connect the church in such a way that it is continually *"being fitted and held together"* and built in love. So many churches today are building in numbers, or knowledge, or programs, or huge campuses. What would it take to change our goals to building love?

APPLY Is there anyone in your church with whom you need to make peace?

_____

_____

_____

What has the Holy Spirit shown you to be your part in increasing unity at your particular church?

_____

_____

_____

How would you describe the relationship between peace, love, and unity?

_____

_____

_____

How can you help your church to build itself up in love?

_____

_____

_____

_____

Extra Mile

PEACEMAKING IN THE CHURCH

Read and study 1 Corinthians 11:27–29. Consider the interpretation that the *"unworthy manner"* mentioned in verse 27 is described in verses 20–22 and judging "the body rightly" in verse 29 refers to the body of Christ or the local community of faith. If this is a correct interpretation, what do you think it implies about the importance of peacemaking in the church?

ABIGAIL—MAKING PEACE FOR OTHERS

Peaceful Hearts

DAY FOUR

There is more to being a peacemaker than being at peace with yourself, with others, and with the body of Christ. A true peacemaker sees conflict between others and is willing to get involved in order to bring God's peace to a war-torn world. Being a peacemaker involves more than letting people have their way. Peacemakers have to see the bigger picture and recognize how self-centeredness leads to conflict. If we help others to identify their own best interests, (which are not always what their self-centeredness desires), the interests of others, and especially the interests of God, it can lead to peace. Abigail is an excellent example of a true peacemaker.

A lot!

📖 Read 1 Samuel 25:2–17. Why do you think Abigail did not do what most submissive wives think they should do? What were her options?

When might a calling to be a peacemaker lead us in an opposite direction from a legalistic perspective?

(what is this?)

1) her servant spoke truth, the men showed respect; her way of life was and safty & others were in jepardy.
2) not much, she could run or tell Nahal.
3) when we think of others before self.

✗ Often our choices are more complicated than a list of rules can address. That is why Christ sent His Spirit to guide us. As a general rule, women can find security in submission to godly husbands, but if they find themselves married to foolish and sinful men, the law of love and peace will sometimes guide them to take action like Abigail.

📖 Read 1 Samuel 25:18–22. What can we learn about peacemaking from Abigail's actions that are recorded in these verses? *She's generous*

She lead!

1) She immediately acted 2) she provided the items needed 3) she didn't include her husband 4) she made decisions on her own 5) she herself went to David

Doctrine

SATANIC FOOTHOLDS

The devil lays snares for people and puts wicked purposes into their hearts. This is, of course, by their consent, or when they leave an opening. But if they resist him, he will flee.[5] When we allow a sin like anger to have a place in our hearts and are not careful to resist Satan, he can gain a foothold that makes it even harder to make peace with and for others.

Notice first that Abigail acted quickly. The longer we wait to make peace the more complicated matters can get. (Ephesians 4:26–27 teaches us to deal with anger before the devil gets a foothold.) Abigail was also willing to take the risk of incurring the wrath of both parties by getting involved. She did not run to her room and hide in self-protection, but intervened with great courage and wisdom. She decided to appeal first to the most approachable party. She knew the character of both David and her husband, and wisely chose to talk with David first. Abigail was also careful to wait to talk with her husband until he was sober. Timing is very important in the peacemaking process.

doesn't say he was drunk.

📖 Read 1 Samuel 25:23–38. How are Abigail's actions a model for peacemakers today? How does her awareness of David's position and interests equip her to appeal to him?

She was willing to intercede on her husband's behalf. She humbled herself

There are three key words that describe Abigail's peacemaking: **Homework, Humility,** and **Honesty.**

Did you notice how much Abigail knew about David? She must have done her homework, and identified and understood who he was, what he was about, what his goals and aspirations were, and something of his character. Philippians 2:4 tells us we should look not only to our own interests, but also to the interests of others. Interests, as understood in this context, are more than the surface issues that are fueling the conflict. An interest is an underlying goal, a foundational value, or a key priority. As we saw yesterday in our study of Ephesians 4, unity in the church is based on the essential doc-

how could you not know about David? How many people held this position?

trines of the work of our triune God. On the surface we can disagree about less important things but our unity is based on the bedrock of our faith. Abigail is obviously savvy to the current political issues yet appeals to David on the basis of his deeper interests of reputation, faith, and desire to do the will of God. If we can help people in conflict to identify their deeper motivations and to live out their higher callings, the road to peace is shorter and not so treacherous. People who find it difficult to agree on surface issues can often find connection on the level of deeper interests. Identifying parallel goals helps us work together rather than against one another.

Secondly, notice Abigail's humility. We cannot emphasize enough the importance of humility in peacemaking. Consider how pride is often an underlying sin in the development of conflict, and it is a no-brainer that humility will be necessary to defuse what anger and pride has built. It takes humility and gentleness to give the soft answer mentioned in Proverbs 15:1. Humility disarms anger.

Finally, did you notice how honest Abigail appears in this story? She didn't try to paint a picture of her husband to make him look better than he was. She didn't make any excuses for him or for herself. She took the blame and gave David the benefit of whatever doubt existed.

Abigail was generous in meeting David's needs and didn't hold back like her husband did, claiming he knew nothing of David—an obvious lie.

📖 Read 1 Samuel 25:39–42. Abigail was willing to be *"a maidservant to wash the feet of my lord's servants"* but David wanted her to be his wife. How does that illustrate the blessing God bestows on His peacemakers?

when we are humble the we show that we are not lord of ourselves, we are not God. it gives glory to God.

James 4:10 tells us God will exalt those who humble themselves. This is one of my favorite paradoxes of Scripture. We think we need to build ourselves up and make our case look good in order to prosper. But God promises to make the peacemakers His sons and daughters. What better prosperity is there?

📖 Read Psalm 27:1–6. What do you think David means by *"dwelling in God's house"*? Contrast that with his statement in Psalm 120:6.

1) in His presence, 2) Those who don't live in His presence.

"A gentle answer turns away wrath, but a harsh word stirs up anger."

Proverbs 15:1

Henri Nouwen, commenting on these verses in his book *The Road to Peace,* writes:

> A peacemaker prays. Prayer is the beginning and the end, the source and the fruit, the core and the content, the basis and the goal for all peacemaking. I say this without apology, because it allows me to go straight to the heart of the matter, which is that peace is a divine gift, a gift we receive in prayer.[6]

APPLY What do you normally do when you see others in conflict? Are you more inclined to stay away from conflict or jump into the midst of it?

ask God what should I do.

What have you learned from Abigail that encourages you to do more peace-making?

Sometimes I jump in too fast, so it would be to humble myself more

What are some deeper interests that you can identify in a current conflict you may know about?

hurt feelings, pride

How often do you pray for peace?

Recall some examples of times when others have intervened in your life to help make peace for you.

Peaceful Hearts

JESUS—MAKING PEACE FOR US

The Old Testament prophet Nehemiah was a type of Christ. Nehemiah's work of rebuilding the walls of Jerusalem was a picture of what Christ would do for His people. His willingness to leave his cushy environment and go to a place of brokenness and war in order to "repair the breaches" was a foreshadowing of the sacrifice Jesus would ultimately make. Nehemiah's conflict with Sanballat, Tobiah, and Geshem not only mirrors the conflict Jesus would have with many of the Jews, but also the struggle we have with those who do not understand and accept the gospel of peace. The prophet Isaiah also points to Christ's peacemaking (and ours) when he says, *"Your people will rebuild the ancient ruins and will raise up the age-old foundations; you will be called Repairer of Broken Walls"* (Isaiah 58:12). Today as you study the verses that describe the peacemaking and mending work Jesus did for us give praise to the Prince of Peace.

Read Matthew 10:34; John 18:10–11; and Nehemiah 4:17. Why is it sometimes necessary to engage in war in order to bring peace? What are the dangers of pacifism? What are the similarities and differences between the swords of Nehemiah, Jesus, and Peter?

We are not called to be door mats. Sometimes to do what God has asked us to do is to fight the enemy; God's enemy. 2) pacifism allows selfishness to continue and to allow ourselves to be not be 10 as children of God. wrongs to enemy be right. stop enemy, be right. 3) Peter's sword was from his feelings. Jesus' sword is fact (this will happen) Nehemiah's sword was defending to self to do the godly thing.

Sometimes peace can only be made by war. Being a peacemaker always entails a willingness and readiness to fight for peace if fighting is necessary to stop evil. John Eldridge writes in *Waking the Dead,*

> The birth of Christ was an act of war, an invasion. The Enemy knew it and tried to kill him. . . . the whole life of Christ is marked by battle and confrontation. He kicks out demons with a stern command. He rebukes a fever, and it leaves Peter's mother-in-law. He rebukes a storm, and it subsides. He confronts the Pharisees time and again to set God's people free from legalism. In a loud voice he wakes Lazarus from the dead. He descends to hell, wrestles the keys of hell and death from Satan, and leads a train of captives free. . . . War is not just one among many themes in the Bible. It is the backdrop for the whole Story, the context for everything else.[7]

Picture the sword of Jesus as the scalpel of a surgeon. Christ uses the sword of conflict to cut away the cancer of sin from our lives. He uses it to separate us from anything or anyone who would keep us from His peace. His motive and timing are always perfect. Christ's first coming did not bring peace to the world, but as we will see in the following verses, it did bring peace to His followers. Peter's sword, however, is an example of inappropriate or untimely "war-making."

Read John 14:27; 16:33; and 20:19. What is the relationship between Jesus and peace? Why do you think the first words He spoke to His disciples after the resurrection were significant?

Peace is connected to love and is Jesus' character. 2) they would think they were seeing a ghost so they would have feared.

Peace is in Jesus. He brought his peace to earth and fought the battle for peace on the cross. Jesus won peace for us and offers it to us within a relationship with Him. The gift of the Holy Spirit brings peace to us. It is a peace that no one and no circumstance can take from us.

Read Colossians 1:17–23. How did Jesus make peace?

by going to the cross, shedding his blood, going to hell. and

The blood of the cross reconciles us with God and cleanses us, making us holy and blameless. We receive peace by faith and continue in peace by continuing in faith. There is no peace without His changing us and making us holy.

We receive peace as a gift. The atonement of Christ on the cross purchases this gift for us, and we receive it at salvation. The Bible calls this justification. Justification is the gift of God's grace through our redemption in Christ Jesus (see Romans 3:24). On the other hand, we experience His peace daily as we are sanctified by the work of the Holy Spirit, convicting, cleansing, and making us holy. We are filled with a sense of His peace when by the power of the Holy Spirit we are enabled to repent, believe, and trust, day by day.

📖 Read Ephesians 2:14–22. What does it mean to you that Jesus is our peace? How did He broker not only peace with God for us, but peace with others who used to be our enemies? What is He doing to maintain peace?

1) Jesus is the covenant (contract) that enables the peace between God + I.
2) Peace is His character and flows through me
3) living in us.

Even though we studied this passage in Day 3, looking at the enmity Jesus put to death in order to establish the unity of the church, I feel it is worth a second look to see how He repairs the walls and builds the temple. Making peace is more than ending strife. It is building common ground. Verses 19 to 22 talk about His building all of us together into a temple—the dwelling place of God in the Spirit. If we could see by faith the reality of these truths, our hearts would be knit together in His love and peace.

📖 Read 2 Thessalonians 3:16. What implications can you draw from each of the phrases in this verse that would help us understand how the Lord of peace grants peace?

ask & it will be given,

Did you catch the significance that this was a prayer, so that peace is granted as an answer to prayer? The word "continually" indicates that this endowment of peace is not a one-time grant. "In every circumstance" implies that we can expect a grant of peace in all of our relationships and in every situation. The final sentence underlines what we have been seeing throughout this lesson that peace is granted through God's presence with us.

APPLY What is your gut reaction to the fact that war often must precede peace? *what is war?*
it can bring things out that want to stay hidden / bring growth maturity,

Do you receive the gift of peace from Christ continually, sporadically, or rarely?
continually

What percentage of your "cup" is filled with peace?
I have peace until circumstances

"Being justified as a gift by His grace through the redemption which is in Christ Jesus."

Romans 3:24

How does what Christ has done affect your ability to find peace with others?

more all the time

What part will Christ have in your making peace with those at odds with you?

Spend some time in prayer before you do anything else. You can use the printed prayer below or write one of your own.

 Father of Peace, I praise You for all You have done to bring me peace. Thank You for sending Your Son to pay the ransom that would purchase peace. Thank You for sending Your Spirit to bring peace into my heart. Thank You for Your presence with me, surrounding me with peace. Thank You for answers to prayer, for bringing peace that passes all understanding, and for guarding my heart and mind in Christ Jesus. You, indeed, are the Great Peacemaker, and I stand amazed that You call me to be a peacemaker as well.

I confess my many failings at peacemaking. Pride keeps me from admitting my own faults that have led to conflict. Self-centeredness keeps me from seeing or caring about others' interests. Stubbornness has kept me isolated. Independence has kept me in disunity. Denial has masked my own hurts and the pain of others. Fear has kept me immobile and unwilling to make peace. I have held on to my resentments and nursed bitterness in my heart, refusing to talk with others about our misunderstandings and barriers to unity. I have avoided some and gossiped about others. And then I blame You or others when I lack peace in my life. Oh, merciful Father, please forgive me. I pray for my family . . . I pray for my friends . . . I pray for my enemies. . . .

Lord, I know the enemy does not want peace, and he is constantly lying and scheming to cause division and conflict. I pray that You would deliver me from his evil intents and change me into a peacemaker. I pray that the way I relate to everyone would bring You glory and extend Your Kingdom. Amen.

Works Cited

1. Ken Sande, *The Peacemaker* (Grand Rapids, MI: Baker Books, 1997), 10, 11, 12.

2. John Newton quoted by John Piper, *The Roots of Endurance* (Wheaton, IL: Crossway Books, 2002), 63.

3. W. E. Vine, *Expository Dictionary of New Testament Words* (Old Tappan, NJ: Fleming H. Revell Company, 1966), 32.

4. Miroslav Volf, *Exclusion and Embrace* (Nashville, TN: Abingdon Press, 1996), 47, 176.

5. R. A. Torrey, *What the Bible Teaches* (Chicago, IL: Fleming H. Revell Co., 1898), 528.

6. Henri Nouwen, *The Road to Peace* (Maryknoll, NY: Orbis Books, 1998), 9.

7. John Eldridge, *Waking the Dead* (Nashville, TN: Thomas Nelson Publishers, 2003), 16.

Notes

Suffering Hearts

"Blessed are those who have been persecuted for the sake of righteousness, for theirs is the kingdom of heaven" (Matthew 5:10)

I actually do not know anyone personally who has experienced physical persecution, so I did some reading and found many books that contain true stories of those who have endured severe persecution for the sake of righteousness. Please check this footnote to get the names of some of the books I recommend.[1] The story I have chosen to share with you is told in the book *Jesus Freaks*. Varia was a young woman growing up in the USSR during the 1960s. Maria, a schoolmate in a Communist boarding school, led Varia to the Lord, and the new convert became an enthusiastic witness for Christ. Varia's courage and proclamation of the gospel led to prison and eventually to a Siberian labor camp. One of the letters Varia wrote to Maria is included in the account in *Jesus Freaks,* and it is reprinted below in its entirety with permission of Bethany House Publishers. The letter illustrates some of the joy and blessing Varia experienced as a result of persecution.

Varia...

...blessing in persecution

My heart praises and thanks God that, through you, He showed me the way to salvation. Now, being on this way, my life has a purpose and I know where to go and for whom I suffer. I feel the desire to tell and to witness to everybody about the great joy of salvation that I have in my heart. Who can separate us from the love of God in Christ? Nobody and nothing. Neither prison nor suffering. The sufferings that God sends us only strengthen us more and more in the faith in Him. My heart is so full that the grace of God overflows.

At work, they curse and punish me, giving me extra work because I cannot be silent. I must tell everyone what the Lord has done for me. He has made me a new being, a new creation, of me who was on the

Here there are many who believe in Christ as their personal Savior.
More than half of the prisoners are believers. We have among us great
singers and good preachers of the gospel. In the evening, when we all
gather after heavy work, how wonderful it is to pass at least some time
together in prayer at the feet of our Savior. With Christ there is freedom
everywhere. I learned here many beautiful hymns and every day God
gives me more and more of His Word.

All our brethren greet you and are glad that your faith in God is so
powerful and that you praise Him in your sufferings unceasingly.

Yours,
Varia[4]

Varia suffered persecution because she refused to be silent about the gospel.
When I compare my hesitancy to say anything about the Lord in the midst
of non-Christians simply out of fear of rejection, to say nothing of actual
persecution, I am ashamed. My prayer is that this study of persecution will
change our hearts and make us more willing to suffer for His sake and to
think more about heaven.

Word Study
PERSECUTION

Persecution is the association of witness and suffering.[2] The Greek word *dioko*, which is translated as *"persecution"* in this Beatitude, means to put to flight or drive away.[3] *Webster's Dictionary* says it means to harass in a manner to injure, grieve, or afflict.

Suffering Hearts

DAY ONE

"*Blessed are the poor in spirit, for theirs is the kingdom of heaven. Blessed are those who mourn, for they shall be comforted. Blessed are the gentle, for they shall inherit the earth. Blessed are those who hunger and thirst for righteousness, for they shall be satisfied. Blessed are the merciful, for they shall receive mercy. Blessed are the pure in heart, for they shall see God. Blessed are the peacemakers, for they shall be called sons of God. **Blessed are those who have been persecuted for the sake of righteousness, for theirs is the kingdom of heaven.**"*

Matthew 5:3–10

JOB—PERSECUTION FROM SATAN

Before we look at persecution from the world we want to take a peek behind the scenes and understand what God has revealed to us about persecution from Satan. Even though we have religious freedom in America and don't experience the kind of persecution seen in other parts of the world, we all experience persecution from satanic powers. It is hard to distinguish normal trials we all face and specific persecution, but as you read the following passages watch for clues that might help us identify persecution from Satan.

Read Job 1:1–12. How do these verses describe Job? What can we learn about Satan's power and limitations from this account? What blessing is implied in being a chosen target of the enemy?

Blameless & upright, feared God. 2) Satan has to ask permission to destroy... do any harm 3) Man of God

Job's faithfulness in interceding for his children is quite impressive. His fear of God and desire for righteousness extended to each member of his family in a way that kept him on his knees, so to speak. It's also interesting to note that God was the one that brought up the subject of Job in His discussion with Satan. Job's life pleased the Lord mightily, and this gave Him reason to make Job a target for Satan. No power struggle existed between Satan and God over Job; God always maintained firm control. But a struggle for truth definitely took place in Job's life. Deception is Satan's prime weapon. He was out to convince Job that God is not to be trusted. When God allows Satan to breech the hedge He has around us, it is always to strengthen our faith, not destroy it. Ultimately, we will be fully compensated for any temporary loss.

📖 Read Job 2:1–10 and 2 Corinthians 12:7. How do you think Paul was so certain that his *"thorn in the flesh"* was a messenger from Satan? Do you think all illness comes from Satan? *no*

Paul knew himself. Maybe God told Paul it was given to him.

Job 2:10 intimates that Job saw his adversity originating from God. On the contrary, Paul states his thorn was a messenger of Satan. But perhaps Paul understood some of the dynamics of the relationship between God and Satan and suffering because he had read the book of Job. I believe there is a danger in thinking that illness and/or whatever suffering we experience can only come from Satan. Such thinking sets up a scenario that suggests a power struggle, and either God is too weak to save us from Satan's attacks, or He doesn't care enough. I am more comfortable in believing in God's sovereign control over all, including Satan. God can allow Satan to buffet us; only God has our own ultimate good in mind when he permits Satan to bring us harm.

📖 Compare Job 4:1–21 with Ephesians 6:11–16. *He does use* How does Satan use the comments of other Christians to persecute us? Why are we tempted to think our battle is with flesh and blood? Where do the fiery darts originate? How do they usually come to us?

1) doubt, jelousy, envy, lack of understanding.
2)

Eliphaz' question in verse 2, *"who can refrain from speaking"* reminds me of James' comments, *"If anyone does not stumble in what he says, he is a perfect man . . . the tongue is a fire . . . and is set on fire by hell."* Eliphaz' accusations against Job in verses 5 and 6 and the description of his dream make it clear that he is a dart in the hand of the enemy. Ephesians 6 teaches us that when we don't have spiritual eyes we see only the person being used by Satan to deliver the darts. God wants us to understand that the real battle is against spiritual forces of evil. When other Christians say or do hurtful things we must be aware of how Satan is using them. We need not fight them, but rather we should look beyond them to see our real enemy.

📖 Read Job 12:9–16 and 1 Peter 5:8–10. Compare Job's description of the origin of suffering with Peter's words. How can we tell if our suffering is from the hand of the Lord or via the attack of Satan? In what ways could it originate from both?

If we take the position that all suffering comes from Satan and must be resisted and prayed away, what happens to our faith when our prayers are not answered? I like Job's approach in 13:15—*"though He slay me, I will hope in Him."* However, we do know from passages like 1 Peter 5 and the first chapter of Job that Satan does attack us. Although we may not be able to comprehend how both God and Satan can be responsible for human suffering, we need to stay in the tension of this paradox. I like what Job says in verse 16 as translated by the New King James Version, both *the deceived and the deceiver are His.* Ultimately, not only are we in the hands of God, but Satan is as well. Nothing can happen outside the will and control of God.

Read Revelation 12:9–12. What is going to happen to Satan according to these verses? How do we overcome him until then?

_____

_____

_____

"Overcoming by the blood of the Lamb" is an interesting phrase. Do you suppose this choice of wording refers to taking communion or maybe having Christ's blood cleanse us from all the sins of which Satan accuses us?

In some ways the other phrase, *"by the word of their testimony"* is even more intriguing. It could be referring to the New Testament, which would encourage us to be women of the Word. Another possible interpretation would be that it refers to the testimonies of others to us, encouraging and strengthening us, which would emphasize our need for community. A third possibility would be our own testimony that overcomes him. One thing for sure, Satan is overcome by our knowing and speaking truth, since he is the deceiver.

The last way to overcome is the most difficult, because it requires the ultimate surrender of our lives. Let's face it; we love our lives too much, and all too often we get tripped up by that love. Hopefully, by the end of this study on the blessings of persecution, we will not hold on to our comfortable lives so tenaciously and will welcome persecution and even death, because death transports us to heaven.

APPLY What suffering have you endured that could have been persecution from Satan?

_____

_____

How does identifying it as persecution help you cope with it?

_____

_____

What blessings did you experience as a result of that persecution?

_____

_____

Do you see yourself as an overcomer?

_____

_____

How much do you think about heaven?

_____

PETER—READY FOR PERSECUTION

Defining persecution can be controversial. Some feel that calling what we might experience in America "persecution" trivializes what other Christians suffer in places without religious freedom. Yet, Paul clearly taught that *"all who desire to live godly in Christ Jesus will be persecuted"* (2 Timothy 3:12). I believe anything that we suffer for the sake of Christ and His righteousness can be called persecution. But I wonder if we should count our religious freedom as a blessing or see it as something that keeps us from the true blessing of genuine persecution. Martin Luther saw persecution as a mark that helps us recognize holy Christian people:

> They must endure every misfortune and persecution, all kinds of trials and evil from the devil, the world, and the flesh by inward sadness, timidity, fear, outward poverty, contempt, illness, and weakness, in order to become like their head, Christ. And the only reason they must suffer is that they steadfastly adhere to Christ and God's word, enduring this for the sake of Christ. . . . Wherever you see or hear this, you may know that the holy Christian church is there.[5]

Peter in his first letter to "God's elect" makes it clear that we are not only chosen for salvation and an inheritance that will never perish, but we are also chosen to suffer. As you study Peter's sobering words, be prayerful that God would strengthen your heart and make you ready for the persecution you have been chosen for.

📖 Read 1 Peter 1:6–9. Why does God allow trials? How do we get to the joy?

1) That faith may prove genuine
2) When Christ is revealed.

Peter's first argument to prove that we should be ready for persecution and anticipate it with joy, is that it will result in praise, glory, and honor for Jesus. Ultimately, that is our goal in life, and we need to see our personal suffering as an opportunity to display God's grace in our lives. We can rejoice in the fact that through it our faith has been proven genuine and our love for Him fills us with glorious joy.

📖 Read 1 Peter 2:18–25. For what purpose have we been called? Why would anyone choose to suffer? What steps are we to follow in responding to unjust suffering?

① to endure unjust suffering ② to show God what they can or would do for Him. Ⓑ because for the will of Christ ③ commit no sin, entrust ourselves to God, no retaliation, make no threats.

The "this" in verse 21 probably refers back to *"bearing under sorrows and sufferings"* in verse 19 and *"enduring it with patience"* in verse 20. If you think about it, Peter's statement is amazing in its scope and very different from the way average Christians in the United States understand their calling. We think we are called to the abundant life. Rather than choosing suffering, we

> "When you do what is right and suffer for it you patiently endure it . . . for you have been called for this purpose."
>
> 1 Peter 2:20–21

suffering good & lead
I choose to suffer for Christ

do everything we can think of to avoid it, expecting miracles to deliver us from any kind of hardship. Perhaps some of our attitudes stem from our reliance upon one of our most fundamental American rights—the pursuit of happiness. Though we should be grateful that we live in a country that protects individual freedom, our mind-set of how God works may need to change if we are to embrace what Peter is teaching here.

Reasons to choose suffering are given in verses 24 and 25. By it we learn to die to sins and live for righteousness. Without suffering we stray. With it we return to our Shepherd and Guardian. John Piper comments:

> Christ chose suffering, it didn't just happen to Him. He chose it as the way to create and perfect the church. He calls us to take up our cross and follow Him on the Calvary road and deny ourselves and make sacrifices for the sake of ministering to the church and presenting His sufferings to the world. . . . We do not choose suffering because it is the right thing to do, but because the One who tells us to describes it as the path to everlasting joy.[6]

Spend some time discussing the particular steps given in verses 22 and 23 that we are to take in responding to unjust suffering. Contrast them with our natural responses. Think of specific examples you have experienced or heard of that illustrate what this might look like.

📖 Read 1 Peter 3:14–17. What specific directions does Peter give in this passage?

> *Do not fear what they fear. Set apart Christ as Lord, always be prepared to give an answer, do it with gentleness and respect. Keep a clear conscience.*

Peter's first direction is *"do not fear."* That seems easy to say, but very hard to do when we are dealing with persecution. John Miller sees unhealthy fear as a heart issue. "When my anxieties dominate and will not go away, I need to face the truth that my devotion is not being given to God with all my heart, but to myself."[7] Peter says that the way to deal with any fear is to set apart Christ as Lord in your heart. If our hearts have been purified to be completely devoted to Him, we can trust Him no matter where He takes us or what He calls us to endure.

Next Peter tells us to be ready to give the reasons for our hope in a meek and gentle way. Imagine yourself in the midst of fiery persecution ready to deliver a quiet, yet powerful defense of the gospel. Then he instructs us to keep a good conscience and to be careful that we always do right. Such a lofty goal makes sense when you see God's goal of bringing the message of salvation to the lost. If we can follow these instructions by the power of His Spirit within us, we will present the gospel in a compelling way.

📖 Read 1 Peter 4:1 and 12–16. How do Peter's instructions help us prepare for persecution? What blessings are promised for those who follow his instructions?

> *1) arm ourselves with same attitude as Christ.*
> *2) Spirit of glory and of God rest upon you.*

"When my anxieties dominate and will not go away, I need to face the truth that my devotion is not being given to God with all my heart."

—John Miller

As Christians, we are to arm ourselves with the purpose of suffering and take comfort in knowing that suffering often turns us away from sin and toward the love of a merciful Father. A tumultuous ordeal lurks just over the horizon (perhaps it is already here), and we will likely be reviled for proclaiming the name of Christ. But we can take joy in knowing that we will be blessed as we eventually pass through the fires of testing and trials. Instead of wallowing in our trials, we are to share in the sufferings of Christ, for we will be blessed in the rejoicing that follows.

📖 Read 1 Peter 5:6–11. What warning and training does Peter give here? What new blessings are outlined?

1) Humble yourselves, cast anxiety on Jesus, be self controlled, and alert, Resist the devil, standing firm in the faith
2) God will restore you and make you strong, firm & steadfast

In our last message from Peter, he warns us to watch out for the devil. We need training in humility, in casting our anxiety on Him, in resisting the devil, and staying firm in our faith. He promises that our suffering will only last a little while (especially in light of eternity, where we will be exalted and enjoy the blessing of utmost bliss in heaven). But he adds to that the present blessing of the work Christ is doing in us to perfect, confirm, strengthen, and establish us.

APPLY After all Peter has said are you ready to choose suffering?

I have

What are some things you need to work on in order to be better prepared for persecution?

not to hold onto offenses, To forgive easily

How has your heart been changed in regard to suffering?

What do you think of this comment from one of my pastors, Kevin VandenBrink?

Failure to embrace the call to suffer leads to a weak and emaciated faith because we never find that God is all we need until we experience that He is all we have.

PAUL—THE PURPOSES OF PERSECUTION

If anyone could fully understand the purposes of persecution Paul would have to be one of them. I doubt any person has experienced more persecution in one lifetime. He even knew what it was like to be a persecutor. Acts 9:15–16 tells us he was chosen to bear Christ's name and suffer for its sake. How we are blessed by being persecuted is one of the seeming paradoxes of Scripture. Consider Mark Shaw's words about paradox.

> If I want to understand the Bible today I need to learn to think in terms of paradox. Christian theology fails when it uses straight-line logic alone. The road to ultimate truth is like a twisting, winding mountain road. . . . God makes things out of their opposite. He makes something out of nothing. He wins by losing. He lifts us up by bringing us low. He works opposite to the way humanity logically expects an omnipotent God to work.[8]

As you study what Paul had to say about both his own persecution and the persecution we should expect and even embrace, be watching for the paradox of blessing.

📖 Read Acts 14:22; 20:22–24; Philippians 1:12–14; 2:17. What do these verses reveal about the purposes of persecution? Discuss ways in which tribulation or persecution can be a doorway into the kingdom of God. Do you think the doorway might refer to the persecution others endure for our sake, as is implied in Philippians 2:17? Whose faith was served by Paul's becoming a drink offering?

_____

_____

_____

In all four of these passages Paul seems to be describing life emerging from the clutches of death, joy from affliction, his continuing distribution of the gospel in spite of his own imprisonment—the great paradox of persecution. I wonder what Paul was thinking when he expected the new believers to be encouraged by his words about tribulation and in what way that would strengthen their souls. It makes me wonder if we as Americans are often spiritually weak because we face so little persecution or refuse to embrace the suffering God brings. Are we bored and apathetic because life is too easy? Finally, take note of the blessing in Philippians 1:14 that came as a result of Paul's persecution, for we will return to this thought later in the lesson.

📖 Read Romans 8:16–18. What is the relationship between suffering and glory? Do you think there is a present experience of glory as well as a heavenly one?

_____

_____

_____

_____

_____

"But even if I am being poured out as a drink offering upon the sacrifice and service of your faith, I rejoice and share my joy with you all."

Philippians 2:17

Paul describes an "if/then" relationship that implies glory is a result of suffering. My first thought would be that the glory will be revealed in heaven and that the "present time" is our time here on earth. But both Larry Crabb in *Shattered Dreams* and John Piper in *The Hidden Smile* of God see a revelation of glory in authentic worship that comes out of our periods of suffering. Consider Piper's quote below:

> Faithful suffering is essential in this world for the most intense, authentic worship. When we are most satisfied with God in suffering, he will be most glorified in us in worship. Our problem is not styles of music. Our problem is styles of life. When we embrace more affliction for the worth of Christ, there will be more fruit in the worship of Christ.[9]

Looking again at verses 17 and 18, I notice that the glory belongs to Christ. We merely share in His glory, and it conceivably could be revealed in us while we worship in Spirit and truth. How we respond to suffering can either bring glory to God or shame to ourselves.

Going back to my first thought of glory revealed in heaven, I wonder if we focus too much on present glory. I don't disagree with what Crabb and Piper point out, but want us to move away from our natural tendency to focus only on the present. What we may experience in worship is only a taste of the glory we will experience in heaven. Just this week my one of my pastors, Michael Kelly, while preaching from John 14:2 and 17:24, said,

> God is not about making life better here, but about preparing us for heaven. Jesus has gone to prepare a place for us. His desire is for us to be with Him there. Everything you want from this world waits for you in the next.

Persecution helps us give up our hope in this world, and put it in the one to come.

📖 Read Romans 5:3–5. What does Paul say here about the purpose of tribulations? What do you think the "hope" refers to?

_____

_____

_____

_____

I wonder if love is our greatest hope, and heaven is filled with love more than anything else? Yes, heaven will be a place of beauty, freedom, joy, and peace, but isn't love what our hearts desire most? If you go back one verse, Paul refers to the *"hope of the glory of God."* But maybe the most glorious thing about God is His love. One thing we do know for sure is that the gift of the Holy Spirit is a down payment of what awaits us in heaven (see 2 Corinthians 5:5), and we are told here He fills our hearts with love.

📖 Read 2 Corinthians 1:3–11. After meditating on this passage, list as many changes to a person's heart as you can find that come as a result of suffering.

_____

_____

_____

"God is not about making life better here, but about preparing us for heaven."

—Michael Kelly

Not only are our hearts comforted, they are opened to trust God more and to love and share with one another more. I see in this passage hearts full of compassion and sympathy for one another. I think our culture's emphasis on individualism keeps us disconnected until some kind of suffering hits, and then we are bonded with those who walk through it with us. Suffering sends us to our knees, both for ourselves and for one another.

📖 Read 2 Corinthians 12:9–10. How can we learn like Paul to treasure Christ more than pain-free living? What does suffering do to our relationship with Christ? In what ways is His grace sufficient for you?

_____

_____

_____

_____

_____

Doctrine
MEANS OF GRACE

The theological term "means of grace" usually refers to a list of provisions God has given that enables us to change and mature in our Christian lives. In most churches it begins with the sacraments of baptism and the Lord's supper, and then includes the Word of God (both its preaching and personal reading and study), prayer, accountability, and in some circles praise and worship. Some churches emphasize the "corporate means of grace" or what we do together in our pursuit of God, and others tend to emphasize more personal pursuit.

Suffering causes us to not only know our own weakness more, but to seek His grace, which leads to His dwelling more fully in us. Our part is to seek His grace. The more time we spend in His presence the more grace we will receive. Taking advantage of all the opportunities to receive grace through His word, in worship, in the sacraments, in prayer, and in fellowship with other believers will help us to grow in grace. Then when God chooses to allow suffering in our lives, we will find contentment in them, as Paul did.

📖 Read Acts 8:1, 4; 1 Thessalonians 2:2; and Philippians 1:14. What blessing comes from persecution according to these verses?

_____

_____

_____

Recently, I read the following prayer request from John Miller's book, *The Heart of a Servant Leader.*

> I have prayed that . . . the truths of redemption become deeply felt realities in our inmost being, that we would hate the sin of apathy in ourselves and others, and passionately love the lost with boldness, tenderness, and brokenness. I want the Spirit to grace me with much patience, a willingness to take each small step necessary to make friends with the lost person, and then boldly stand before the heart's door and knock. And then to stand with tears before the person's inner citadel and plead for the lost one to grab hold of the only salvation there is. The Father must give much new grace if this is to happen. I am often so far from this kind of total commitment to the Lord Jesus. Pray for me, my brother, pray for me![10]

I believe one of the primary results of persecution is a growing sense of the urgency of spreading the gospel. Just as the brethren in Rome were given courage to speak the word of God without fear as a result of Paul's persecution, we are awakened and emboldened to share the truth we know in the midst of any experience of suffering. Maybe all the "new grace" that is given carries a bonus gift—a passion for the lost. Persecution and suffering take us to the core realities and the important priorities. May His kingdom come and His will be done!

APPLY Paul gives us the following purposes for suffering. Put a checkmark next to the ones which are most compelling for you.

❑ provides a doorway into the kingdom
❑ bears His name before kings and nations
❑ helps us let go of selfishness
❑ helps us testify to the gospel of grace
❑ leads us to being glorified with Christ
❑ opens the door to intimacy with Christ
❑ leads us to comfort
❑ helps us trust more
❑ teaches us endurance
❑ helps us to connect more with others
❑ causes us to pray more
❑ causes us to know our weakness and seek His grace more
❑ resets our priorities

When was His grace most sufficient for you?

_____

_____

_____

Do you suffer from affluenza (spiritual illness stemming from materialism) or apathy? How might a little persecution be the antidote?

_____

_____

_____

Do you need more passion for the lost? Are you inclined to pray like John Miller? Why or why not?

_____

_____

_____

TAMAR—THE PERSECUTION OF WOMEN

Suffering Hearts
DAY FOUR

Webster's Dictionary defines persecution as the act of persecuting those who differ. Today we are going to focus on persecution of women by men. We first need to discern if this type of persecution has anything to do with being persecuted for righteousness's sake. I believe it can when men persecute women because women reflect a different part of the image of God.

■ Women whose hearts have been renewed reflect the beauty of the Lord, and unrepentant and insensitive men persecute them when they take advantage of their beauty rather than honor it

- Women whose hearts have been renewed reflect the meekness of Jesus, but men sometimes persecute them by using their strength and leadership role to dominate and control
- Women whose hearts have been renewed reflect the "helper" model of God, yet some men persecute women out of pride because they cannot bring themselves to accept help from women
- Women whose hearts have been renewed reflect the compassion and nurturing side of our heavenly Father, and sinful men persecute them by hardening their hearts and driving them away
- Women whose hearts have been renewed reflect the desire for intimacy of the Holy Spirit, and men in their sin withdraw and hide from connection

When a woman experiences persecution from a man, she is, in a sense, sharing in the sufferings of Christ, because the way the man treats her is ultimately a reflection of his heart toward God. If a man abuses the beauty of a woman, he has never learned to honor the beauty of the Lord. A dominating man does not understand Christ's teaching on meekness. A man who withdraws from relationship with his wife has first hidden his heart from God. Women, by their differences, can threaten and bewilder men. In the worst cases, sinful responses to the differences can lead to misogyny (the hatred of women), homosexuality, pornography (false intimacy without connection), rape, abuse, divorce, and other forms of persecution.

Where is the blessing of such persecution? The blessing comes when we turn to Christ in our grief and refuse to respond negatively to the persecution. When we continue to reflect the beauty of the Lord, we share in Christ's honor. When we continue to respond in meekness, we share in His rest. When we continue to offer our help and our gifts, we share in His reward. When we continue to show compassion and long for intimacy, we find it in His arms. As you study and discuss the story of Tamar, I invite you to grapple with the reality of the persecution of women and find the blessing Christ has promised.

📖 Read 2 Samuel 13:1–9. How and why does beauty invite persecution? How do the actions and words of Amnon and Jonadab make you feel?

_____

_____

_____

Men like Amnon blame women for their beauty and claim their seductive ways give them no choice but to carry out their lust. Some women can recognize men's self-centered, deceitful schemes and learn to avoid dangerous situations and are disgusted by such disgraceful behavior. Others, like Tamar, are caught in the traps of wicked men.

📖 Read 2 Samuel 13:10–15. What do you think of Tamar's words and logic? Why do you think Amnon refused to listen? Why did he hate her?

_____

_____

_____

Tamar's statement that *"such a thing is not done in Israel"* probably refers back to the incident in Judges 19 and 20 when God revealed His wrath over

Extra Mile
PERSECUTING MEN

Knowing women sin just as much as men, think of ways some of our most common sins might be a type of persecution of men seeking to reflect the image of God:

- rebellion
- discontent
- independence
- usurping authority
- control
- manipulation
- disrespect

the sin of rape. The fighting men of Benjamin were virtually wiped out because they did not turn over some rapists to the rest of the nation of Israel who, like God, were incensed over the rape and death of one man's concubine. The deaths of twenty-five thousand men for one woman provide a pretty strong deterrent to rape.

Hatred and blame shifting are the usual ways of dealing with unrepentant guilt. If lust made Amnon sick in the beginning, his guilt made him even sicker once the sex act was over. Tamar was left with the consequences of both sickness and guilt. As you discuss this part of the story, consider the question, "Why do women often have to pay for men's sin, and carry the shame of sexual abuse?" As you think about this, consider the importance of mourning, forgiveness, and sharing the suffering of Christ.

📖 Read 2 Samuel 13:16–22. Why would sending Tamar away be a greater wrong than rape? What do you think of Absalom's words and David's inaction?

_____

_____

_____

_____

Amnon's hatred and rejection cause deep wounds in Tamar's soul that will take much longer to heal than her physical pain. Absalom's telling her not to take this to heart seems insensitive and so out of context. Her father's refusal to deal justly with the whole sordid affair may be the most painful response and certainly led to the most destructive consequences. Unresolved conflicts are always a cancer that can destroy families, churches, and nations. Tamar is left to grieve alone, and even the author never returns to tell us what becomes of her.

📖 Read Malachi 2:13–16. First of all, please notice the footnote in the New American Standard Bible that identifies the literal meaning of the Hebrew word for divorce in verse 16. Compare that "sending away" with what Tamar experienced. If you insert the literal meaning and study the context, whom does God love and show His great concern for in this passage, and what does He hate?

_____

_____

_____

_____

I first came to understand this passage after hearing a widow speak on how the Lord had become her "husband" like He promised the Israelites in Isaiah 54. She brazenly said that this promise in Isaiah 54 could be applied to widows, but not for women who are divorced, because "God hates divorce." I knew she was wrong, because I had experienced His promise, and I was divorced. So I went to Malachi, and asked God to show me what the verse really meant. Now I am challenging you to do the same.

The wording _"deal treacherously"_ is repeated three times in this passage, and it gives us a strong hint as to what is making God so angry. His love is not for the institution of marriage, and His hatred is not for everyone who fails

Word Study
SENDING AWAY

I find it extremely intriguing that the literal meaning of the word usually translated "divorce" is actually "sending away." This is what Amnon did to Tamar. It is also the meaning of "persecute" according to _Vine's Dictionary_—the Greek word _dioko_ which is translated into English as persecute means "to put to flight, or drive away."[11] I believe the application of this verse is much broader than divorce. It could include emotional "sending away" so common in many marriages. It is what men who fear intimacy do repeatedly.

to stay married. His love and concern is obviously for the women who have to endure treachery. It is for the Tamars who are sent away. His anger is against the men who fail to love their wives, who use violence, and abuse, and send their women away.

Can you see how some have taken the statement "God hates divorce" out of its context and used it to force women to stay in abusive marriages? Think how that is the very opposite of the point of the whole passage.

📖 Read 2 Corinthians 4:8–10 and 16–18. What is a proper response to persecution? How and when are we blessed?

_____

_____

_____

_____

There is no "happy ending" for Tamar. Sadly, this is true for many other women as well. The blessing we are promised does not guarantee that the men in our lives will change. Like Paul we may continue to experience affliction, perplexity, and persecution. The key for us is to respond as Paul did. Don't let this study take you into men bashing or tempt you to hate them all. Don't let men crush you, or cause you to despair. Don't take on the identity of being forsaken, because Christ has promised to never forsake you. No man can destroy you. Remember that you are not only made in His image, you carry in your body the death and resurrection of Christ, and He will be manifested in you as you live for Him. Don't lose heart! It is being renewed! The light affliction you are experiencing is producing for you an eternal weight of glory!

APPLY Has this study helped you to understand the suffering you have experienced at the hands of evil men in terms of persecution? In what ways?

_____

_____

In what wrong ways have you responded to persecution by men, and how would you respond today?

_____

_____

_____

Why is it important for you to forgive those who persecute you?

_____

_____

Where is God, and what is He doing in the midst of our persecution?

_____

_____

"Blessed are you when men cast insults at you, and persecute you, and say all kinds of evil against you falsely, on account of Me. Rejoice, and be glad, for your reward in heaven is great, for so they persecuted the prophets who were before you."

Matthew 5:11–12

WALKING WITH JESUS

We open today's lesson with the following quote from John Piper:

> What a tragic waste when people turn away from the Calvary road of love and suffering. All the riches of the glory of God in Christ are on that road. All the sweetest fellowship with Jesus is there. All the treasures of assurance. All the ecstasies of joy. All the clearest sightings of eternity. All the noblest camaraderie. All the humblest affections. All the most tender acts of forgiving kindness. All the deepest discoveries of God's Word. All the most earnest prayers. They are all on the Calvary road where Jesus walks with his people.[12]

How often do we refuse to walk with Jesus because we want to avoid suffering above all else? Avoidance of suffering is part of the American creed that many in the church have signed onto. Such a pervasive attitude is certainly not biblical, and as Piper points out, we lose some of the greatest blessings available to mankind by fearing suffering and running from it rather than embracing it. As you read and study the following passages, keep in mind the blessings we miss when we turn away from walking with Jesus out of our fear of suffering.

or how do we pray for the suffering to stop in others & our lives?

📖 Read John 15:18–21. Why does the world hate Christians? What risk do we take when we walk with Jesus? What do you think it means to suffer *"on account of Me"*?

1) Because they hate Christ. 2) Of being hated - persecuted 3) to be hated because my belief in Jesus.

I see four reasons Christians are hated revealed in this passage: 1) the world hates Christ; 2) we are different; 3) we are chosen; and 4) the world does not know God. When we walk with Jesus we risk the same kind of treatment the world gave Him. It is our identification with Him that brings out rage and persecution in many. If we would denounce His name the persecution would surely end.

It is Christmas time as I write this and every night we hear in the news of more efforts to take Christ's name and incarnation out of the "Holiday" celebration. Many of those who hate Him will not rest until His name is erased, so they do not have to hear it.

📖 Read Philippians 3:8–11. According to verse 8, what is Paul's rationale for walking with Jesus? What happens as a consequence of his decision and how does he respond? What fellowship is found in sharing the act of suffering with Christ?

1) surpassing greatness of knowing Jesus Christ
2) Paul loses everything and considers all rubbish
3) Become more like Christ in His death.

If you were Paul, how would you respond to the consequences he faced in walking with Jesus?

- ■ I would fight to hold on to my stuff (it certainly is not all rubbish)

- ■ I would consider his chosen lifestyle to be a bit too radical

- ■ I would try to figure out a way to enjoy life both now and in the here-after

- ■ Since intimacy with Christ seems unattainable I would settle for less

- ■ I really want to respond just as Paul did

Did You Know?
THE 10/40 WINDOW

The 10/40 window is the area between the latitudes 10 degrees and 40 degrees north of the equator and between the Atlantic and Pacific Oceans. This rectangle approximates to the areas of greatest spiritual challenge to the gospel. The countries in or near the 10/40 Window are the most under-evangelized in the world. Over 95% of individuals who have never had the chance to hear the gospel reside in the Window area.[14]

Paul wants to know Jesus above all else, so he is willing to suffer any loss in order to walk with Him and know Him better. All the things we might consider necessities of life Paul considers rubbish. He must have so treasured the intimacy, the righteousness, and the power he experienced in his walk with Jesus that everything else faded in significance. The phrase *"conformity to His death"* makes me think of Paul's treatise in Romans 6 where he explains how we can die to sin by being united with Christ in His death. Walking with Jesus takes us to the cross, but it is there we are freed from the bondage to sin.

📖 Read Hebrews 13:12–16. What do you think *"the camp"* is, and what is the difference between a lasting city here and the city that is to come? What practical things must we do to carry out these instructions?

1) The world 2) here on earth vs after Jesus comes? 3) praise (confess His name) to do good and share with others (maybe tell other)

I believe *"the camp"* is a comfortable place of living and belonging. *"Outside the camp"* is a place of persecution—maybe like the "10/40 Window" (see sidebar for explanation) or a part of the city you live in that needs the gospel. We seek a *"lasting city"* here, as our time and money are spent in an effort to increase our affluence and make this temporary home as much like heaven as we can. But those who seek "the city which is to come" sacrifice their earthly goods and time to focus on praising God, confessing Christ's name, doing good, and sharing with others.

John Piper says it best:

> The call of Christ is the exact opposite of retreat. Since we have no lasting city here, stop working so hard to make it lasting and luxurious, and "go forth to him outside the camp"—outside the safe place, outside the comfortable place . . . Let go of what holds you back from full and radical service—be ready to suffer for finishing the Great Commission.[12]

📖 Read Matthew 5:12, 6:20, 19:21 and Psalm 16:11. What kind of reward do you think He is referring to? How and why is it ours?

1) Our reward will be to be with Jesus in heaven for eternity. 2) it is ours because we are His - we believe

The recurring phrase in each of these passages is "in heaven." We usually think of reward here on earth in terms of money or material gain. But if you think a bit further, we use the money and possessions to bring joy and pleasure. Whatever the rewards are, we know they will bring eternal joy and pleasure.

📖 Read Revelation 21:22–25 and 22:3–5. What do you think it means that the nations will walk in His light? In what sense will our walk with Jesus never end?

1) Be in His presence 2) we will be with Jesus for always

All our fear of walking with Jesus will vanish in heaven. There will be no risk, no darkness, and never a time when we can't see what is ahead. The apostle John sees the Lamb as the temple, the sun, the moon, and the glory of heaven. We will always see Him, always bear His name, always serve Him, and will reign with Him forever and ever.

 APPLY Do you fear walking on the Calvary road of love and suffering? What holds you back?

I ask God to remind me during the suffering that something good will come out of this.

In what ways have you been persecuted on account of Jesus? Share an account of both the pain and blessings it brought.

_____

_____

_____

_____

What fellowship with Jesus have you experienced in the midst of suffering?

_____

_____

Is your goal to make a lasting city here or a better one there?

_____

Do you long for heaven? What stands in your way?

No I long for others to be in heaven with me.

_____

Close your time together in prayer.

Father, we thank You for renewing our hearts. Who would have thought at the beginning of our study that we would come to embrace poverty, mourning, meekness, hunger, mercy, purity, peacemaking, and persecution? But Your Word and Your Spirit have worked miracles in our hearts, and we thank You.

Lord, we know Your work is not yet complete. In some ways it has just begun. Please prepare us for the days ahead. As we experience more and more persecution, we ask that You would make us ready and willing to stand for the truth and glorify You by all we do and say. Please forgive our fear, doubt, and timidity. Give us strength, faith, and boldness. We are so comfortable here, and hold tight to our luxurious lives rather than seeing ourselves as strangers and aliens. Forgive our unwillingness to suffer, and give us eyes to see that better place, the heavenly city, and help us to store up treasures there.

We pray for deliverance from the evil one. May he not deceive us with his lies or defeat us with his accusations. Help us to sing with Martin Luther:

A mighty Fortress is our God, a Bulwark never failing;
Our helper He amid the flood of mortal ills prevailing.
For still our ancient foe doth seek to work us woe;
His craft and power are great; and, armed with cruel hate,
On earth is not his equal.

Did we in our own strength confide, our striving would be losing;
Were not the right Man on our side, the Man of God's own choosing.
Dost ask who that may be? Christ Jesus it is He.
Lord Sabaoth his Name, from age to age the same,
And He must win the battle.

And though this world, with devils filled should threaten to undo us,
We will not fear, for God hath willed His truth to triumph through us.
The prince of darkness grim, we tremble not for him;
His rage we can endure, for lo! his doom is sure;
One little word shall fell him.

That Word above all earthly powers, no thanks to them, abideth;
The Spirit and the gifts are ours through Him who with us sideth;
Let goods and kindred go, this mortal life also;
The body they may kill: Gods' truth abideth still;
His kingdom is forever. Amen.

Works Cited

1. Randy Alcorn, *Safely Home* (Wheaton, IL: Tyndale House Publishers, Inc., 2001). A novel based on true accounts of persecution in China. An interesting read because the author imagines some of the blessing and reward that awaits the characters in heaven, as well as the blessing they experience in the midst of persecution.

—DC Talk and The Voice of the Martyrs, *Jesus Freaks, Stories of Those Who Stood for Jesus: The Ultimate Jesus Freaks* (Minneapolis, MI: Bethany House Publishers, 1999).

—John Foxe, *Foxe's Book of Martyrs* (Uhrichsville, OH: Barbour Publishing Company, 1989).

—Douglas Hsu, *Voices in the Wilderness, 100 Uplifting Stories From God's People in Different Lands* (Charlottesville, VA: Advancing Native Missions, 2001).

—Paul Marshall, *Their Blood Cries Out, The Worldwide Tragedy of Modern Christians Who Are Dying for Their Faith,* (Dallas, TX: Word Publishing, 1997).

2. J. D. Douglas, organizing editor, *The New Bible Dictionary* (Grand Rapids, MI: Eerdmans Publishing Co., 1973), 968.

3. W. E. Vine, *Expository Dictionary of New Testament Words* (Old Tappan, NJ: Fleming H. Revell Company, 1966), 3:177.

4. DC Talk, 101.

5. Martin Luther, *Martin Luther's Basic Theological Writings* (edited by Timothy Lull, Minneapolis, MN: Fortress Press, 1989), 561–562.

6. John Piper, *The Dangerous Duty of Delight* (Sisters, OR: Multnomah Publishers, 2001), 83.

7. C. John Miller, *The Heart of a Servant Leader* (Philadelphia, PA: P&R Publishing, 2004), 66.

8. Mark Shaw, *10 Great Ideas from Church History* (Downers Grove, IL: InterVarsity Press, 1997), 23.

9. John Piper, *The Hidden Smile of God* (Wheaton, IL: Crossway Books, 2001), 169.

10. Miller, 76.

11. W. E. Vine, *Expository Dictionary of New Testament Words* (Old Tappan, NJ: Fleming H. Revell Company, 1966) 3:177.

12. John Piper, *Don't Waste Your Life* (Wheaton, IL: Crossway Books, 2003), 76.

13. Piper, *The Hidden Smile of God,* 170.

14. Ralph Winter and Steven Hawthorne, *Perspectives on the World Christian Movement* (Pasadena, CA: William Carey Library, 1999), 543.

Notes

Notes

May 1   wk 8   Day 1 + ②

May 8   ③

May 15   4 + ⑤